MICHAEL MORAN

Michael Moran is a nice enough chap of middling height who made a number of bearable, but not remotely successful records in the Eighties and Nineties. None of them were about holidays. He has written for *Arena*, the *Face*, and *The Word*, and is now a journalist for *Times Online*. He is not expecting a promotion to the travel section any time soon. He has co-authored three books: *Rock and Pop Elevens*, *The Encyclopædia of Guilty Pleasures* and *Shopping While Drunk*.

Sod
Abroad

Why you'd be mad to leave the comfort of your own home

MICHAEL MORAN

JOHN MURRAY

First published in Great Britain in 2008 by John Murray (Publishers)
An Hachette Livre UK company

I

© Michael Moran 2008

A CIP catalogue record for this title is available from the British
Library

'Holiday Rap' Words and Music by Bruce Welch, Brian Bennett,
Curtis Lee Hudson and Lisa Stevens
© 1986, Reproduced by permission of EMI Music Publishing Ltd
trading as Elstree Music, London W8 5SW

ISBN 978-0-7195-2140-9

Typeset in Trump Mediaeval by Servis Filmsetting Ltd, Manchester

Printed and bound by Clays Ltd, St Ives plc

John Murray policy is to use papers that are natural, renewable and
recyclable products and made from wood grown in sustainable forests.
The logging and manufacturing processes are expected to conform to
the environmental regulations of the country of origin.

John Murray (Publishers)
338 Euston Road
London NW1 3BH

www.johnmurray.co.uk

For Cassie:

This is better than a duty-free giant Toblerone, isn't it?

Contents

Introduction: The Glove on the Railing (or why civilisation stops at Dover)

We Britons have for centuries enjoyed an international reputation for decency and fair play. This is no time for false modesty: the British are quite simply the finest people on earth. That's why, according to a recent Home Office estimate, upwards of 170,000 people a year apply to join this joyously inclusive club. Here's the reason: walk down any British street and you'll see a glove on a railing. That's our flag, not that garish red-and-blue affair you sometimes see made into boxer shorts. The glove on the railing betokens a belief in civilisation that you just won't see anywhere else in the world. It says: 'Somebody has lost a glove. I don't know that person, but I want them to know, should they return this way, that someone cared enough about their well-being to lift their mitten out of the muck.'

Still, travel agents, bless their avaricious little hearts, spend their entire working lives trying to convince us that we should spend our annual fortnight of freedom in some frankly rather inferior country that doesn't *have* any gloves on its railings. You'll never see a beret on the fence along some Parisian boulevard. Indeed, some of these other places vying for our two weeks are too warm for anyone even to *wear* gloves. You don't need upstarts like me to tell you that it's unwise to venture into any of these apparently tempting locales – with no gloves to serve as a barometer of social decency, how can we be sure that we're amongst right-thinking people? Limiting one's excursions to resorts within these sceptred isles is scarcely the safer option either: the British countryside, with its dearth of railings, offers few indications as to the innate decency of the locals. Best, then, to remain safe within the confines of our cosy market towns or, ideally, one of the great conurbations, as most Britons live in built-up areas for one perfectly simple reason: if it were worth living anywhere else, we'd have built our cities there instead.

In this book, I have listed more than a hundred reasons why you should never waste another penny on a holiday. There's even an equation. If just one of these reasons can convince you to try slacking about in your front room for a fortnight next summer, I've done my job.

13 things you will forget to pack

1 That Book You Really Wanted To Read
There's this thing you saw on *Richard & Judy* once that sounded brainy and entertaining at the same time. It's a hardback, though, and they weigh a *ton*, so there's no reading it on the way to work. No. It's a 'save for the holiday'

book. It'll probably make it into the case* for a bit, then get taken out to make room for some flip-flops and never quite find a place in your hand-baggage. So, assuming you brought your glasses, you'll end up making do with some flimsily unsatisfying paperback humour title you found in the airport WH Smiths instead. This is it, actually, isn't it?

2 Reading Glasses

Brainy people like you and me read a lot. We tend, therefore, to wear out our eyes and page-turning fingers a great deal more quickly than the common-or-garden thickies who are planning to spend their holidays in the *Big Brother* house without so much as an eye chart to read. We don't want to draw too much attention to how far we've eaten into our life expectancy, though, so whereas we'll be making room for at least a *couple* of pairs of sunnies, some subconscious vanity will make us leave those vital close-work goggles on the bedside table.

3 Contact Lens Solution

Brainy as we are, we don't know the Thai for contact lens solution, so we've got no chance of buying it while we're

* Incidentally, packing books into your hold baggage is rather frowned upon by airport security staff. On the mysterious scanning devices they use to inspect your luggage, a book will look like a suspicious black oblong. It would never occur to them that someone would take a *book* on holiday, so they will assume you're a terrorist with a block of exotic explosive and destroy your bag in a controlled explosion just to be on the safe side.

away. Even if we did, we'd probably end up getting palmed off with some counterfeit muck containing a flesh-eating acid left over from a Chinese bioweapons research programme. Ally that to the current sensitivity about transporting liquids on airliners, and the perfectly natural tendency to forget things that are a bit on the dull side, and you have yourself another optically challenged fortnight.

4 Nail Scissors

Well, they aren't going in hand baggage, for a start, and that's where all the other things that get remembered at the last minute end up. And there's effectively no chance of remembering to put them in your main suit-case. Don't go looking in your complimentary sewing kit either. There won't be any *there*. Who knew your toenails could grow so much in a fortnight? Those sensible walking shoes will be agony by the end of week one as your toenails begins to scythe viciously into the adjacent soft tissue every time you take a step. Let's hope you packed some sandals. You did, didn't you?

5 Umbrella

Let's face it, it's going to piss down.

6 That Thing That Charges Up Your iPod/Mobile/Camera

It probably won't plug into the ridiculous unearthed deathtraps that Johnny Foreigner favours anyway, but when you need to listen to some music to take your mind off the whole ghastly experience, call your mum to tell her you weren't involved in that riot she saw on BBC News 24 or to gather evidence on your cockroach-infested hotel room so you can sue the tour operator, you'll need to suck up some electricity from somewhere, as it's beyond the scope of current technology to design a battery that can go for ten days without recharging. Even if you switch off your mobile phone between uses, it chews through so much electricity playing that ridiculous tune every time you switch it back on that the battery will be a spent force long before you can call your mum up to ask her if she can remember the name of your hotel when you're drunk in a gutter in Prague. Solar panels? Don't make me laugh.

7 Tampons

The mighty cosmic clock that powers the universe is the last thing you'll be thinking about when you're trying to find space in your case for a couple of spare thongs and a straw hat, but Arsenal's home fixtures are as inconveniently reliable on holiday as they are terrifyingly tardy that first nail-biting month after you get back.

8 Condoms

Single or settled, you wouldn't want to jinx your chances by taking a box of johnnies. It looks a bit too much like you're expecting some action. If you're a man, everyone will think you're a bit presumptuous, and if you're a woman, there's always the danger that what everyone in Britain sees as 'empowered' everyone in Athens will see as 'a trifle loose'. Therefore, a box of prophylactics is something you'll accidentally on purpose forget to pack on the assumption that you can get some while you're away if things *do* take a turn for the fruity. What you may, of course, overlook is that, if you buy condoms in any Catholic country (and a surprising majority of the more popular holiday destinations share that distinction), you can never be sure whether or not they have been secretly perforated with a bodkin by an excessively devout shopkeeper.

9 Telephone Number Of The Credit Card Fraud People

The minute the Czech waiter clocks your English accent, he'll be jabbering in some ridiculous language on his stolen mobile to a couple of pals in the Russian Mafia and they'll have your card cloned before you can say 'Two more Budvars, please' in your halting phrasebook Slovak.

10 The Perfectly Legal And Acceptable Ointment For Your Athletes Foot/Eczema/ Piles

Not glamorous, but essential. This is the one thing you might be best off forgetting, I suppose, because you can bet your life that, as soon as they catch wind of something mildly embarrassing in your suitcase, the customs officers will be on to it like a dog on bacon.

11 Hangover Remedies
It would be too straightforward for German chemists to stock a nice packet of Resolve like civilised people. The expression you're looking for is 'Ich habe einen Kater'. Don't say I didn't try to help.

12 The Address For Logging On To Your Work Email
You sort of more or less remember most of it, but you'll still end up wasting three quarters of your Internet café time typing in random letters to see if you can get lucky.

13 Proper Drugs
We'll be talking about illegal drugs in detail later, but according to my *Sunday Times*, a worryingly large percentage of people in the UK are taking them. And, frankly, even if you didn't before you clambered aboard the plane, you'll be desperate for something to numb the pain by the time the pilot says 'cabin doors to manual'. But don't imagine for one minute you can buy any dirty street gear in the bog standard tourist trap *you're* going to. After all, you never see Pete Doherty at Euro Disney, now do you?

Drink: The easy way to endure your partner for two weeks

It's easy to argue on holiday. For a start, you've got the time – normally, any fully-fledged domestic disagreement has to be scheduled into those rare moments between work and sleep, and therefore rarely reaches a truly satisfying conclusion. We rarely argue at home because, in real life, time is at a premium. On holiday, frankly, you've got too much of the stuff.

Once we have established the opportunity, we need only discuss the motive. There are, of course, seven possible flashpoints:

Pride You think you look ineffably *chic* in your new holiday shorts/sarong/sunglasses. Your spouse will almost certainly disagree.

Gluttony Another profiterole seems like the most reasonable idea in the world. To you and you alone.

Sloth You appear to have inadvertently gone on holiday with the kind of person who wants to *do* things on holiday. Day trips and such. That isn't a rest, it's a prison sentence.

Envy That couple in the next chalet may earn more than you, may have a nicer car than you, may have better-behaved kids than you, but they needn't give you such pitying looks. That's just nasty. And there's no need for her to agree with them.

Jealousy That waiter was *definitely* looking down her top. Definitely.

Avarice She fancied a boutique hotel. You thought a camping trip would be better value. More fool you. You're going to spend two weeks arguing. In a tent.

Wrath Well, of course you're cross. See above.

There is only one guaranteed prophylactic against such a conflict leading to the ruination of your holiday and, by extension, making the most expensive thing you'll buy all year a complete waste of money. It's alcohol.

I know what you're thinking: in the UK, alcohol is the root cause of most, if not all strong differences of opinion outside licensed premises. This is because we tend to start drinking far too late in the day and, therefore, alcohol-induced surliness takes hold before its essential corollary, booze-led torpor. On holiday, however, we apply a formula known to scientists as The Tippling Point: because drinks are fed steadily into the bloodstream from lunchtime onwards, the body becomes gently tranquillised, leading to an all-pervading *longeur* that leaves the subject incapable of anything more assertive than, for example, the composition of French symbolist poetry. At home, drink will lead to your undoing. Overseas, it is your saviour.

Of course, you're still best off not going at all, but if you *must*, a powerful thirst will be your greatest ally.

11½ absolutely awful holiday records

The key to a holiday record, especially a truly awful holiday record, is to have a little bit of 'language' on it. It doesn't have to make any sense to anyone; holiday record lyrics are developed by the same top language scientists that make up preposterous euro-isms like 'Tresemmé' and 'Nutrisse' for the cosmetics industry. The eleven and a bit records below are not so much music as aural viruses transmitted by easyJet. You've probably heard all of them. You probably hoped you had forgotten them. Here are some unwelcome reminders:

'Agadoo': The holiday record that has it all – a clodhopping beat you really can't avoid wedded to instructions that you can follow even after seven or eight of those lovely mauve cocktails that they only do 'over there', *and* an incomprehensible title. 'Agadoo' is one of those records that everyone you meet will profess to hate, but which still manages to sell a zillion copies.

'Encore Un Fois': A bit of a cheat, this one – A fairly standard club galloper, punctuated by occasional panicky shouts of something French. A bit like those telephone conversations you have with Continentals who speak perfect English, but you still can't resist yelling 'Bonjour!' at at the end. Yes, it's quite as bad as that.

'The Birdie Song': Admittedly, there's no language in this one, except for the European lingua franca of irksome tweeting. It has actions, though. They're compulsory. One of those holiday gems that was in the Top 40 twice in the same week, even though no one bought this one either.

'The Macarena': There's some proper Spanish in 'The Macarena', distilled into an amiable gibberish by its legions of copiously refreshed devotees. *And* there are actions. If that wasn't enough, the woman who burbles away in the middle sounds like she might be fairly fruity, although she probably only wants to marry you to get UK residency or something.

'Saturday Night': Pure evil on disk, this record will burrow into your brain like one of those worm thingies in *Wrath of Khan*, except there's no Captain Kirk coming to save you from Whigfield.

'Y Viva España': Most holiday records at least pretend to achieve their status by some happy accident. Not so 'Y Viva España'. There should be some sort of international accord about the cynical targeting of excessively *slaked* clubbers with such perfectly designed holiday records. It's got language aplenty, with Spanish and English lyrics sung by a Swede for that irresistibly pan-European flavour.

'The Ketchup Song': Language wrapped in a tongue twister layered over a pilled-up Steely Dan out-take. Culturally, it's as nourishing as the toxic condiment from which the song takes its name.

'Una Paloma Blanca': Another holiday monster that charted for two different artistes, the best known being, of course, the unwisely bewigged celebrity jailbird Jonathan King. 'No one can take my freedom away' went the refrain. He probably believed that when he sang it.

'Going to Barbados / Going to Ibiza': A record that, in its two guises, displays very different aspects of the holiday song. In 1975, only a few British people would have been able to afford a holiday in Barbados, and the message of the song – aside from a gentle hint of happy-go-lucky racism – is ultimately aspirational. In 1999, when the Vengaboys disinterred the remains of the track and stitched it crudely back together, everyone in Britain had already been to Ibiza, necked the pills, applied ointment to the rash and moved on. In the 1975 version, there's no language as such, apart from some ill-conceived accent work, but the Vengaboys cunningly remedied this oversight by pronouncing 'ee-beet-za' in the oddest way imaginable.

'The Lambada': It's *all* language. No one knows what it's about, but it provided the soundtrack to a thousand and one ill-conceived Shirley Valentine moments involving ladies of a certain age and amoral Greek waiters on the make. They all ended in tears and so, for most lovers of good music, does this record.

'Holiday Rap': (by MC Miker G and Deejay Sven) The motherlode. It would be the easiest thing in the world to get a few cheap laughs by just quoting (out of their carefully crafted artistic context) some of the more embarrassingly awful lyrical content. So that's exactly what I'll do*:

* Before you start feeling guilty about mocking their somewhat casual acquaintance with the English language, bear in mind that I – and, by extension, you, the valued purchaser of this book – will have to pay MC Miker G and Deejay Sven (or their appointed representatives and creditors) a moderate sum of money for the privilege of quoting their lyrics. In addition, I daresay numerous other authors of mildly amusing books about bad English, music, holidays or bad English holiday music will have had much the same idea and so I would imagine Miker and Sven (I think we can afford to be reasonably familiar, we *are* paying their mortgage this month) will be, on balance, pretty happy with the whole situation.

We took a holiday with all our friends.
It was a time to relax and let your worries behind
Exactly seven weeks or something crossed my mind.
It was the shine of the time we never forget

Fair enough they're Dutch, and English isn't their first language, but my message to them, and to anyone else essaying a little bit of 'language' to promote a cosmopolitan air, is this: when you are speaking 'in foreign', you will *definitely* sound stupid. So don't do it.

Who are you going to believe? The man who just wants £7.99 from you or the chap who's after a grand?

No matter what the travel industry, with its sinister vested interests, might have you believe, there's no certainty that that expensive holiday you've booked will be the wonderfully idyllic and restful affair described in the advert. Equally, to be fair, it's not *absolutely* certain that you'll be evacuated home from your holiday sweating deliriously from force ten food poisoning or a rare malarial infection, or both. Nor can I guarantee you'll be defrauded, pickpocketed or thrown in jail for being an unwitting drugs mule either. But you *might*. And why would any sane person take that risk? You could avoid even the possibility of a mediocre couple of weeks in a mildly disappointing resort, only to come home to appreciate just how nice your home actually is, by just not going anywhere in the first place.

Which is, I think you'll agree, easily done.

My point is that there's only one way a holiday can go right, viz. the pleasant sojourn advertised in the brochure, and a couple of hundred ways it can go wrong, as will be enumerated in this book. Forewarned is forearmed. Or, better still, forewarned is cancelled and spending a very nice couple of weeks slacking about in the home that you would appreciate more if only you could first go and catch diphtheria in a badly run campsite somewhere where they still have wolves.

Mick Jones of The Clash once asked me, and the several hundred thousand other purchasers of the *Combat Rock* album, whether he should stay or whether he should go. I never got around to answering Mick, but I'm giving you the advice I should have given him: you should stay. It's better than you think. And the other place is worse.

Sarongs: Why?

An easy one to clear up. In the original Malay, the *first* syllable is silent.

Baggage handlers: Your life in their hands

The baggage handler who found a camel costume in someone else's valise is rightly the stuff of legend. One dull day in Sydney airport, he happened to open one of the suitcases in his care, found a camel head and, *of course*, he put it on. Who wouldn't? Wearing an unexpectedly discovered camel head is the birthright of every right-minded Australian. But hang on – are we expected to believe that he opened *one bag at random* which *happened* to contain a comedy camel head? Of course not. A big score like that can only be the fruit of months, perhaps years of optimistically opening strangers' luggage, most commonly to be rewarded with nothing more entertaining than some mildly amusing underwear, or some pile ointment. The crowning achievement of the camel head proved also to be the last for our puckish baggage handler, however: he was seen dancing comically around the airport, wearing the unique ship-of-the-desert-style headgear, by (of all people, what are the chances?) the very owner of the aforementioned ruminant disguise. Bad luck for him, good luck for every news researcher looking for a mildly amusing 'and finally' to sweeten the grim realities of the ten o'clock bulletin. Quantas never named the playful miscreant, so there's no way of ascertaining his current occupation. Perhaps he's working for another airline? Perhaps he found his true vocation as a customs officer? Who can say? It matters not.

The real issue is that, for every light-hearted suitcase chucker caught with his hand in the Samsonite, there are dozens (perhaps scores) who are just as inquisitively amoral, but smart enough not to get caught. The holiday is typically a time when our notions of privacy relax a little: we write postcards rather than letters, giving everyone in the sorting office an insight into our vacation activities; we might disport ourselves on topless beaches, even if we are the kind of people who, at home, might never, no matter how well the cheese and wine is going, reveal our feminine charms for our neighbours' collective gawping pleasure. The luggage issue, though, is less consensual and strangely more personal. All right, we probably pack (or forget to pack) much the same stuff as everyone else, but the issue is that it's *our* generic Gap boxers, M&S bra and Agent Provocateur spanking paddle, and we don't want them messed with.

One might think that the answer might be to lock the cases, perhaps with one of those handy straps that tend to be sold by small airport concessions positioned in that corridor just *after* you've checked in. That would be a mistake. To a customs officer, a locked bag is a suspicious bag. He (or she, there's no gender bias when it comes to pure evil) will take great pleasure in breaking open the case on the slightest pretext, irrespective of the harm it might do to fine quality plastic zips, buckles and straps.

Of course, ultimately, it's all our fault. At the time of the infamous 'camel head' incident, an unnamed Quantas baggage handler was quoted as saying that of *course* they didn't open the bags, because they simply didn't have *time* to search every bag*. One might be forgiven for asking how he knew that unless he had tried, but all of this demonstrates one thing: the only safe place for your luggage is on top of your wardrobe, where it belongs.

Holiday reading: The thicker the better

You're clearly the kind of person who is quite discerning when it comes to literature. In daily life, many people are. When it comes to *holiday* books, though, suddenly weight becomes the main criterion. Everybody seems to want something that will, irrespective of its literary merit, push them over the excess baggage limit, so let's face the awful truth about holiday books: *they are there to take your mind off the holiday*. That's why they are selected for page count rather than quality. There are four

---

* 'Every now and then a bag will fall open, sometimes because it is poorly secured; but more often it is because the bag itself is cheap, faulty, overloaded or all three.' Yeah, right, pal. That's *exactly* what happens.

main categories of holiday read, one to weight down each corner of your beach towel, and they are:

Celebrity Autobiography Perhaps the most inaccurately named of our categories, celebrity autobiographies are invariably anything but. Most of the celebrities invited to jot down the outline of their rags-to-riches tale are entertainers and sports folk who devoted most of their school years to practising karaoke or keepy-ups rather than acquiring literacy skills and so are obliged to employ that bitterest of individuals, the ghost writer. Ghost writers are generally quiet, bookish souls who were persecuted by those very popular kids at school who went on to become football players or in a boy-band or something. The fact that the ghost writer is *still* doing their homework for them twenty years later is a humiliation scarcely ameliorated by the fee paid, which, although apparently a tidy sum of money in itself, always works out to an hourly rate marginally less impressive than you could get for assembling sportswear in Phuket. Every one of these books that you buy supports this appalling exploitation. *And* you'll only read the bit where they got addicted to Haliborange or whatever and then the rest of the holiday the book will be just be used to stop your towel blowing away. You should, therefore, boycott all celebrity biographies forthwith. I would like to add at this point that this book was compiled under strict Fair Trade guidelines. I've had that Bono round to check.

Gun Porn The popular choice for the gentleman holidaymaker. Generally written by one of those two blokes who were in the same not-very-well-organised SAS mission. Or the late Robert Ludlum. As young lads, most men, unless they were destined to grow up to be ghost writers, read a fair amount of Commando Picture Library comics interspersed with the odd Dorling Kindersley affair featuring cutaway drawings of nuclear submarines, or aircraft carriers or somesuch. Gun porn is essentially a textual cocktail of the two, except with a couple of subplots and a bit of brutish fruitiness thrown in to fatten the book up and compensate for the lack of diagrams.

Chick Lit The history of women's popular fiction is a long and noble one, taking in such greats as Jane Austen, Mills & Boon and Dame Barbara Cartland (all of whom have published comforting stories about downtrodden young women who, despite considerable adversity, always manage to marry a nice young man). Chick Lit is pretty much the same stuff but with some extra bits about shoes to make the books a touch thicker and more holiday-compliant. To make it easier for the hurried shopper to identify Chick Lit, there's invariably a drawing on the cover that looks like a panel from George and Lynne. Premium offerings may also have a bit of glitter glue on the front. And because even the thickest Chick Lit novels can fail to pass the holiday bulk test, they are frequently bundled in bookshops' 'Buy one, get nine free' offers and so represent excellent savings, which can then be spent on shoes (v. good). Even allowing for such superb value, though, Chick Lit is a *bad thing*, because it discriminates against women who can't afford lots of shoes, or those among us who are (and I mean this in a sisterly way) unavoidably bootfaced and unlikely to marry a handsome doctor. They'll probably end their days shacked up with a ghost writer, poor dears.

Pop Science You'll read the title, sure enough. It'll be something irresistible like *Time Machines and Ray Guns: How To Build Them In Your Shed*, but as soon as you get past Chapter 1, it's all quarks and gluons and line drawings of something that *could* be a molecule, but might just as well be the solar system, or equally, now you look at it again, it's quite possibly a loose pile of Haliborange. Either way, it'll give you a headache, but because you don't want to be thought of as the kind of unconscionable thickie who was playing keepy-ups when you should've been learning about atoms, you'll have to accidentally drop it in the pool with a theatrical sigh of disappointment.

So there you have it. Give or take a three-inch-thick slab of fantasy hokum called something like *The Seven Fire Dragons of Winchelsea* (from the effectively interminable Chironex trilogy) to cater for the genuine oddballs, that's all the choice you're going to get. If you were to stay at home, you could perhaps leaf through an enchantingly slim volume of gentle humour. In fairness, I'm probably not the best person to advise you there . . .

TRAVEL TIPS #1:
THE MIDDLE EAST – How to be a loveable hostage

First, some historical background. In the Bronze Age, the Middle East, as it is today, was a hot, dry, inhospitable place populated by some very imaginative and excitable people. Because, in the Bronze Age, these people were generally undernourished, dehydrated and, by our standards, poorly educated, it wouldn't be surprising if, through a mélange of superstition, confusion and hallucination, they developed some very peculiar ideas about theology.

Fortunately, the area was, in those days, also home to at least one talkative and omnipotent deity who dispensed advice and occasional manna to the locals, leading to at least three of the top five hit religions starting up in the area.

So far, so good. Unfortunately, many of the adherents of these religions believe, perhaps correctly, that the best way to spread peace, love and tolerance is by shooting one another. That's a shame, because the Middle East is, after Waitrose, the best place to get a really nice orange. So what does this mean for you, the potential Middle East holidaymaker? Well, I can't guarantee that you'll *definitely* encounter one of the great variety of religious fanatics with AK47s in the area, and even if you do, I can't *promise* that you'll be abducted, but (like having clean pants on in case you get hit by a bus) it's as well to be prepared, just in case. There are four distinct grades of armed menace in the Middle East – here is a handy guide to the key differences between them:

The Soldier Clean-shaven. Will shoot you if you in any way resemble someone he doesn't like.

The Insurgent Is a bit stubbly. Doesn't get as much rifle practice as his clean-shaven counterpart, so may well shoot you if you are standing *near* someone he doesn't like.

The Freedom Fighter Has a moustache. Idealistic. Might shoot you, but is a bit short of cash and so would therefore prefer (ideally) to kidnap you.

The Terrorist Same as the freedom fighter, but has a beard.

Realistically, you're more likely to be shot or blown up than kidnapped, but I can't help you much with those. If you *are* kidnapped, though, make sure you remember Stockholm Syndrome. Not, as you might reasonably imagine, an inch-thick Robert Ludlum paperback, it's a term describing the congenial bonhomie that ensues when a group of idealistic gentlemen with beards are sequestered for any length of time together with a nervous young backpacker. You might think that the best way to engender this bonhomie, which, after all, may aid the continued retention of your head, is to be terrifically pally around your captors and offer to do the washing up etc. Unfortunately, Middle Eastern culture (very sensibly, in my view) makes use of a good deal less cutlery than we do. Therefore, there's a *lot* less washing up, so try to think of some other way of making yourself helpful around the house while still remaining manacled to a radiator. Better still, just get your oranges from Waitrose until these various young men of varying opinions and levels of shavenness have sorted out their differences. They've been arguing for about five thousand years, it can't be *much* longer.

Aeroplanes: They're just common, aren't they?

The appeal of air travel is rooted in a spurious 1960s notion of glamour involving well-groomed people hopping on and off Concorde – people who are, on the one hand, entirely unaware of problems like noise pollution and their colossal carbon footprint but, on the other hand, are carrying really nice little blue bags with BOAC written on them. The truth today is far more democratic and infinitely more ghastly. Every few minutes a chubby little orange-and-white aeroplane takes off from one of the airports clustered around London, packed to bursting point with people who are unlikely to be able to eat, drink or satisfactorily visit the lavatory for over an hour. They will be flown at speeds well in excess of 500 mph to assorted destinations around the world that have become more English than England itself by dint of the current cheapness of flying. International journeys have become nasty, brutish and short.

There are some worthy souls who are very much opposed to the popularisation of air travel. They will point out that British emissions of CO_2 from air travel shot up from a far from acceptable 4.6 million tons in 1990 to a somewhat disquieting 8.8 million tons in 2000. That's a lot. If a loved one emitted 8 million tons of gas during Christmas dinner there would be questions asked, let me assure you. It gets worse, though. With the queasyJet lifestyle still expanding (the current annual figure of 180 million sweaty tourists is expected to rise to something like 476 million even *sweatier* tourists per year by 2030), our gaseous emissions will probably be more like 18 million tons in 2030. It's enough to make the most sanguine Range Rover owner a little concerned. Don't worry yet, though, as it's about to get even worse: aircraft emissions that go directly into the stratosphere have, my boffins tell me, at least twice the harmful effect of emissions from cars or power stations at ground level and (based on some calculations our government paid for on our behalf, because we're all interested) the effect of the 2030 emissions will be equivalent to a positively unsettling 44 million tons of carbon. That's enough to worry Clarkson.

Some people don't have time to worry about the ecological effect of air travel because they're too busy worrying about the plane crashing, though. In fact, this is very unlikely. Statistically, the chances of an average person being involved in a major aircraft accident are close to nil. You probably already knew this, but the most dangerous part of any international journey ends when you leave your car in long-term parking. One you're aboard the plane, you're probably safe. It's not all good news, though. Also statistically, the chances of spending the next hour or so trapped in a metal tube full of strangers' farts and eating terrible, terrible food while potentially fatal blood clots accumulate in your legs are, in defiance of some natural laws, a little over 100 per cent.

The original appeal of air travel was based on its exclusivity. Over the last twenty years, it has become one of those exotic commodities, like cappuccinos, cocaine or ciabatta, that have regrettably trickled down as far as the tracksuit wearing classes. Consequently, a trip on a modern airliner is like an extended wait in some vast cylindrical dole office. When the mile high club throws open its doors to people with elasticated waistbands, it is time, my friends, to leave the club.

THINGS YOU CAN
ONLY DO @ HOME #1:
Taking drugs

Depending on which edition of *Mixmag* you last read, anything between 16 and 105 per cent of adult Britons regularly use illegal drugs. Irrespective of your own predilections in this area, it's generally accepted that the only differences between legal and illegal recreational drugs is one of historical fluke. An historical fluke that the current government is, at the time of writing, attempting to remedy by making tobacco illegal as well.

Whereas a wayward minority of drug users may get themselves into something of a pickle, drift into petty crime and generally clutter up the tabloids, for most the discreet after dinner spliff or line is as much a part of British culture as Chicken Tikka Masala or sun-dried tomatoes. And most drug users rub along nicely as responsible members of society and merely employ certain proscribed substances to unwind at the end of a stressful working week.

So, when they go on holiday, these people might reasonably expect to unwind a little further (after all, they don't have to get up in the morning and the most common side effect of drug abuse is an aversion to alarm clocks) – except they can't. The downside of taking drugs for fun is the obligation it confers upon one to enter into commercial transactions with petty criminals. Now, British petty criminals are by and large splendid fellows, always ready with an amusing anecdote about their time in chokey and quite happy to go along quietly should they regrettably be arrested in the course of their daily work.

The Continental criminal is an altogether rummer cove. With his shifty eyes and questionable hygiene, any Spaniard might be taken for a drug dealer. And, indeed, with virtually every Spanish-issued Euro note being encrusted with residual blow, he may as well be. However, one can't simply bowl up to some randomly selected picaroon and inquire as to whether he might have any 'gear' or 'muck'. That really would not do; drug slang is a constantly evolving beast and staying on top of even the British euphemisms is more-or-less a full-time job. So just imagine the magnified complexities of the inter-national translation of such terms. And, as yet, unfor-tunately, there is no international body engaged in the European harmonisation of drug nomenclature. Besides, even the most unkempt Frenchman might possibly be involved in the comic operetta that our European cousins imagine will pass for law enforcement.

Yes, there are holiday locales famed for their mind-altering amenities – Ibiza, Aya Napa and certain parts of Latin America come to mind – but the act of buying drugs in such a location is likely to involve a great deal of sleight of hand and will more probably than not leave you in pos-session of a bag of somewhat overpriced talc.

Equally, for reasons that we will address elsewhere, the notion of transporting illegal drugs though HM Customs is a temerarious venture, only to be undertaken by such dashing privateers as – and here I select just one example at random – Sir Paul McCartney. It's quite one thing telephoning a man called Chad or Bradley* when one is sequestered in one's own rooms and inquiring as to whether he has any class C smokeables, it is quite another to walk past armed police with a sachet of what may or may not be oregano in one's hand baggage.

So, the one time of year when a person might most be in a position to enjoy a prohibited substance is the time most likely for that same person to have no chance whatsoever of obtaining one. Now, I'm not actually suggesting that you substitute a fortnight's cycling tour of Provence for two weeks on your sofa in a marijuana fug, but it's a compelling alternative, isn't it?

Swimming: 5 reasons never to do it

No matter what certain oddball science types would have you believe, man is a land animal. It has been

---

* There is an esoteric branch of criminology which explains that it is not christening a child with an exotic name that will lead him into a life of crime, it is merely that they are the only kinds of name one might be able to remember at 2 a.m. when the craving for a Toblerone is only surmounted by the feeling that one last reefer might see one off to bed nicely.

demonstrated more than once that not only should humans not spend excessive periods of time in water, they shouldn't even run alongside pools containing the vile stuff. Ducking, bombing and diving are similarly prohibited. The following five admonitions should be taken together as a final proof, as if proof were needed, that swimming is *not* for the likes of us:

1: At least since the end of the last Ice Age, and one would most fervently hope during it, most decent people have worn at least *some* clothing. There's a very good reason for that: no matter how impressive a naked person might appear in a dimly lit bedroom environment this evening, their flaws would be all too apparent should their nude body be pressed against the window of a crowded commuter train during tomorrow morning's rush hour. A swimsuit offers precious little dignity to the average physique. Until such time as tailors develop a well-cut pinstriped suit that will bear protracted immersion in salt or chlorinated water, I must counsel against swimming on grounds of public decency alone.

2: If you immerse yourself in a swimming pool, it will almost certainly contain a mild solution of chlorine, the substance used, to widespread disapprobation, by the German army as a gas weapon during the Great War. Sea water has a more variable chemistry, depending on your location. Typical constituents are chloride, sodium and a goodly amount of raw sewage. People don't shower after a swim for fun. It's because whatever liquid in which you choose to swim is likely to be hazardous and / or vile.

3: Your fingertips aren't supposed to go all wrinkly like that. Unless you're planning an elaborate jewel heist tonight and can't find any gloves that match your mask, there is no earthly reason to disfigure your fingertips thus.

4: Unless you've found a vast lake of Ambre Solaire to swim in, swimming will inevitably have the effect of removing any sun protection with which you have been have anointed. Because of the cooling effects of the water, you could be forgiven for not noticing the inimical solar radiation until you are already really quite burned, which as we all know is too late. Yes, there are indoor pools, but the noise level in them is invariably deleterious to the sanity of all but the hardiest or deafest of swimmers.

5: We will deal elsewhere with some of the frankly rather nasty denizens of the sea, but I managed to make it all the way through that section without once raising the topic of the candirú, a translucent (almost invisible) river fish which lodges itself in the human rectum or urethra and then deploys bony spikes to anchor itself there seemingly out of sheer spite. Evolution has provided man with a partial defence against this evil creature by instigating dramatic penile shrinkage when the body is immersed in water. It doesn't last long, but, nevertheless, male readers will be acutely aware that when the gentleman's gentleman is at his most visible, he is paradoxically at his least impressive. All the more reason to sequester oneself, fully dressed, in one's conservatory with a selection of fine wines. Now *there* is a liquid-based pastime of which I can unreservedly approve.

Blagging an upgrade: Impossible? Yes!

The free upgrade to First Class is the number one urban legend of airline travel. Everybody knows somebody who *knows* somebody who *met* somebody who once heard about somebody *else* who shared a cab with someone who told *them* about getting bumped to First*. Conversely, every check-in clerk knows that there will be at least one chancer per flight who will sidle up to the desk, shuffle nervously from foot to foot for a moment and utter the time-honoured phrase 'I don't suppose there's any . . . err . . . chance of, um . . .' before scuttling back to those

* Probably the same apocryphal individual who had their arm broken by a swan's wing. That's never happened either; it's just a story that swans put about to make themselves look tough.

uncomfortable benches that are placed in the economy lounge to remind people like you that, even though you're not on the plane yet, it's never too early to get numb buttocks.

Of course the answer is no. Unless you are a vicar, or your surname is Branson, it's better not to ask. After all, given that you already know the answer, do you *really* want to give the clerk the satisfaction of refusing you?

Anyway, only perhaps the great Noel Edmonds could successfully pass himself off as a long-lost Branson brother, through you could always *dress* as a vicar . . . Let's analyse the top five 'sure fire' methods of ensuring yourself an upgrade:

1: Carry a wedding dress. Out of the question for (at least) 50 per cent of readers, this relies on the ability of an impending wedding to soften the heart of the check-in clerk. Pure fantasy. They've seen it all before. Nothing weaker than radioactive nitric acid will affect that flinty organ in their chest.

2: Wear a nice suit. At least achievable for most. The downside is that, should you fail, or more correctly, *when* you fail, you will have condemned yourself to 90 minutes in a cramped economy seat while wearing the least comfortable yet most expensive garments you possess, knowing that neither you nor your suit will be improved by the experience.

3: Have nice luggage. Not a cheap option. A really good suitcase will cost you a fair chunk of change. And will spend most of its life collecting dust on top of your wardrobe. Unless you travel a lot, it might be cheaper just to pay for a better airline ticket. Especially as there's no guarantee that the clerk will notice your case unless you're balancing it on your head, which can tend to offset the classy look you're going for. Remember also that the baggage handler, that magpie of the conveyor belt, can never resist a Louis Vuitton bag.

4: Have a title. Remember, though, the people you're trying to convince have just looked at your passport, and the Queen tends to get fairly cross with people who make frivolous alterations in their passports. 'The Very Reverend' is your best bet: it implies that you won't get carried away when the free champagne comes around. Baronets among you may find that, for obvious reasons, their title has almost exactly the opposite effect.

5: Be famous. Of course, many famous people can afford an upgrade anyway, and by buying an economy seat and banking on the bounce to save a few quid, you're risking the ignominy of not being recognised at check-in and being condemned to flying with a bunch of commoners who almost certainly *will* recognise you and not give you a moment's peace – especially if that episode of *Never the Twain* you did when the mortgage was overdue comes on the in-flight video.

Given the impossibility of the task, and if you still insist on going away on holiday, it's probably best just to turn up at the airport in your special 'flying' tracksuit with your 'benefit tartan' blue-and-red laundry bag and accept whatever woefully cramped seating you are allotted. At least that way you are assured of a quiet dignity that the upgrade chasers will never have.

Why you can't get Dundee cake in Dundee

I can't explain this one. I'm sorry; I've tried but it just can't be done. You can't say I haven't done my research. Waitrose do a nice one, if that's any help, *and* they deliver to your house. So maybe that's where you should be?

THINGS YOU CAN ONLY DO @ HOME #2: Watching proper telly

Of course foreign telly is rubbish. That's a given. Let's not even mention non-English-speaking telly. That would be like shooting fish in a deep fat fryer. Let us instead focus on the country that is, let's be honest, the source of some of the finest shows that we are offered by British broadcasters: *The United States of Rome* and *Sex and the City* (and *The Sopranos*). Even if your hotel 'don't got' HBO, there *should* be a sufficient amount of entertainment on American TV to fill those desperate hours when you woke up too early and just can't get to sleep.

Should be.

Unfortunately, some weird alchemy occurs when the advertisement-to-content ratio edges past 77 per cent: it's just impossible to remember what's going on from one minute to the next. Even simple fare like *Star Trek*, renowned for being easier to follow than *Balamory* and more plausible than *EastEnders* (although, then again, what *isn't?*), is transmuted into some sort of Turner Prize video installation by the reckless admixture of a surfeit of important messages about Chicago's biggest furniture warehouse and its Labor Day reductions. For the weary traveller already addled by the psychotropic effects of jet lag, the threat to mental health is well-nigh incalculable.

Camping: All the comforts of homelessness

You may know that the earliest cities were, until recently, thought to have been founded in ancient Sumeria (now rebranded with the more tourist-friendly name of 'Iraq') around three or four thousand years BC. If you are particularly *au courant* with affairs archaeological, you may also be aware of digs in the Ukraine, which suggest that mankind's transition from a sort of prehistoric crusty Peace Convoy nomad to a respectable urban dweller began significantly earlier. If you knew about those already, well done, but I feel obliged to warn you now, before you read any further, that you're probably a bit too brainy for this sort of book. Nobody likes a show-off.

Anyway, since those crude beginnings some 15,000 years ago, cities and the buildings within them have steadily grown in size and sophistication. It takes a troubled mind, then, to deliberately ignore mankind's steady progress since the Stone Age and plan a *holiday* conducted under mildewed canvas. Although the golden age of campsite misery was probably sometime in the 1970s, there are still such troubled minds abroad in our fair land today. Troubled minds with beards attached. Troubled minds with beards, a misplaced notion that a miserable holiday is, perforce, an economical one and the makings of a mildly depressing bivouac.

The countryside is a sort of picturesque factory for vegetables and cows and so on. It looks quite nice from a train, as long as you're going fast enough. The factory owners, who are sometimes known as farmers, make a tidy sum from growing the above mentioned foodstuffs. Sometimes they even make a tidy sum by *not* growing foodstuffs. (This is known as the rural economy, and it's *far* too complicated for a little book like this.) Nevertheless, bits of countryside have been set aside for the gullible to pitch tents on. This isn't because the campsite owner is a philanthropic soul who wants everyone to share in the clear air and green grass of his bucolic idyll. It's because he's a shiftless yokel who would rather sit on his rustic rump and collect money for nothing rather than doing anything tiring like farming. There are refugee camps in parts of Africa and Asia where hundreds, sometimes thousands, subsist in Bronze Age conditions and most people are quite properly outraged that this still occurs in the twenty-first century. Irony indeed, then, that many of these same quite decent people spend considerable sums of money in replicating these unconscionable conditions in Devon, or the wetter parts of France. And there's some strange alchemy around a sizeable acreage of stretched canvas that attracts rain like a picnic attracts wasps. The sun may be only 93 million miles away but, when you're camping, let me assure you it seems a good deal further.

The only two nods to modern life on a campsite are a communal shower complex, which doubles as a verucca exchange, and the occasional bacon sandwich prepared over a tiny blue terrorist stove thingy which always looks as if it's just *itching* to explode. These fleeting pleasures aside, though, camping is a grim business. Don't be deceived by propaganda films like *Carry On Camping* – your correspondent once spent two sodden weeks on the Isles of Scilly and not a single bra flew off. Indeed, every man, woman and child on those benighted islands was so thoroughly swaddled in gender-masking sweaters, cagoules and sou'westers that there was no possibility of directly observing any underwear at any time. Not even one's own. The only benefit of such a holiday is the feeling of sheer relief on returning to your home, which one hopes would feature comfortable furniture, a refrigerator and at least a modicum of shelter from the elements, all impossibilities on a campsite.

If anyone *ever* suggests a camping holiday, I urge you to treat them with sympathy, not violence – however justified it may seem. Simply sit them down with a cup of tea and explain very carefully that the Neolithic era is now over, that we have buildings and respectably large settlements to live in, and that they needn't have nightmares about mammoths anymore.

TRAVEL TIPS #2:
ENGLAND – They're not 'reserved', they really *do* hate you

You and I have probably never met*. Nevertheless, I can confidently aver, in the potentially career-ending style of

---

* Unless, of course, I've just signed this little book for you, in which case, yes, that *is* my actual handwriting and, no, it can't be helped. Thanks for popping by, though.

the young Jools Holland, that, if you've read this far, you are almost certainly something of a groovy fucker. However, even the grooviest among us need some sort of respite from the endless round of star-studded parties, red carpet premieres or (in some cases) soul-destroying office jobs that are our quotidian lot, and it can sometimes be that, when we are feeling at our most weary, we can, *in extremis*, be tempted by the notion of renting a cottage in the shires.

Let us be clear: despite the name and wide variety of strange little people, Middle England is nothing to do with *Lord of the Rings*. Middle England is not so much a location as a state of mind. Like Bertie Wooster's idyllic milieu wherein aunts are the most dangerous people that one might encounter and the two World Wars never happened, so Middle England is a temporal portal to the days before Britain achieved the strength in diversity that makes us undeniably the world's top nation. Unfortunately, Middle England is also the place where all the really nice tea shops are.

The price of a really nice pot of Earl Grey and some delicious homemade lemon cake is an awkward half hour in a café filled with *Daily Mail* readers who, even though all their clothes were purchased by mail order from the *Radio Times*, feel, inexplicably, that they're better than you and that they're going to look at you, mutter to each other and tut ostentatiously until you do the decent thing and scuttle back home to the unconscionable urban ghetto from which you sprang.

The fact that the overpriced cream teas that you and people like you buy every weekend have financed the dry stone walls that they have built around their monocultural Ambridge of the soul in no way ameliorates their innate distaste for anyone who they suspect of harbouring an innate grooviness.

Suntans: Fashion at its deadliest

It wasn't so long ago that a suntan was the badge of the underachiever: it betokened a life of unrewarding back-breaking toil in (somebody else's) fields digging up turnips or loganberries or somesuch. The quality would sequester themselves in their towers – which, contrary to reports, were rarely (if ever) made of ivory – and cultivate a pallor which allowed their veins to shine through the skin in azure splendour. Hence the expression 'Blue Blooded'. And also the expression 'shiftless aristocratic parasite'. Thanks almost entirely to the efforts of fashion designer, Nazi collaborator (well, they did have those *darling* little hats) and *parfumier* Coco Chanel, this centuries-old order was overturned in the mid 1930s. All of a sudden, everyone wanted a tan, and was, if need be, willing to travel a considerable distance in order to get one. In one of those historical ironies that make the writing of slim volumes of humour a ridiculously easy job, at almost exactly the same time the demand for agricultural labour began to fall off and most of us were herded into call centres and egg factories* and the like. I don't know enough about the Industrial Revolution to say exactly why that was, though. Perhaps loganberries just went out of fashion? My essential point is that the suntan went from being the natural concomitant of a working life to the prized accessory of an idle one.

But, the deep and crisp and even tan of the bikini model is not a thing to which the average individual might realistically aspire. The impossibility of applying sunscreen at exactly the same thickness all over the body leads almost inevitably to a charmingly Friesian appearance. Anyway, even if you had a perfect all-over tan, what would you do with it? Lapdancer and *Big Brother* contestant are pretty much the only two careers that involve enough public nudity to make all that sunbathing worthwhile, and they're both pretty hard to get into. You probably need exams or something.

It should also be remembered too that the acquisition of the perfect natural tan is something of a project: too much sun too early and you face the danger of a first-day burn, necessitating days sequestered in one's rooms

---

* There really *are* egg factories. What exactly is made in these edifices, bearing in mind that even a lifelong urbanite like me has heard of hens, is something of an enigma. I intend to address this mystery in a future book.

waiting for symptoms to abate before sunbathing can continue; leave it too late and you risk the ignominy of returning home to questions about poor weather. Tanning on a beach dictates that you shower every evening to remove sand, and rinsing the mouth free of the ghastly grit with a good deal of Continental lager. Tanning by a pool obliges one to endure the company of the sweaty walrus-like Germans and annoying Italian teenagers that infest every expanse of open water between Calais and Antarctica.

Of course, the real reason why a suntan might not be the cleverest thing to get is the alarming rise in the incidence of malignant melanomas since the dawn of the package holiday era. Of all the laughably suicidal pastimes on offer, sunbathing has now overtaken smoking as the most popular and the most deadly. One may well feel the need to ask oneself, when considering the above: 'Am I willing to risk death in order to get something which lends me an evanescent sense of wellbeing, when, after all, 80 per cent of it will be hidden under my clothes for most of the fortnight that it will take to fade forever?' One might also consider that a similar sense of wellbeing can also be achieved simply by having a nice cup of tea. And perhaps a biscuit. Apart from its consoling qualities, tea contains antioxidants which may prevent cancer, as opposed to suntans which do everything they can to promote it (most biscuits don't do much either way, but they're ever so nice).

It's as bad as you think:
Club 18-30

Herded relentlessly from hangover to crudely sexual beach game to pub crawl, oppressed by the knowledge that it will all happen again tomorrow, while being constantly harangued by club reps to fork over extra cash for a ride in a coach delivering sixty shrieking blotchy-legged Peterborough shopgirls with skin peeling from their tattooed tits to an even *more* desperate club night (*marginally* further from your holiday resort) that's about as authentically Tunisian as Arctic Roll. And you've *still* got a hangover. Some people take home a nice bottle of olive oil. Some people take home a stuffed donkey. At the very best, all *you'll* have to show for your expensive holiday is a love bite. Oh yeah, baby. You're in the *jet set* now.

Fear and Loathing in
Las Palmas

Over the last half century, southern Spain has become the holiday destination of choice for millions of British tourists. Basically, it's as far as you can go towards the searing heat of the equator without having to deal with the unremitting *foreign*-ness of African or Asian destinations. Since the middle of the 1980s, though, Spain's coastal regions have become occupied by an invading horde even worse, if you can imagine this, than the Spanish: it's us.

The first wave of colonisation was benign enough: Conference League gangsters on the lam, a smattering of Sangria Socialists who moved before the memo on Tuscany became policy and a rag-tag army of crystal-toting New-Agey fantasists with Venus in the ascendant and luggage in transit.

Then it got nasty: a veritable infestation of unctuous Thatcherite estate agents, swimming pool salesmen, land-grabbers, carpetbaggers, bull-necked skinhead chancers and leather-skinned swingers turned up and dug in, rubbing their hands in gleeful anticipation of the next batch of exploitably naïve arrivals. They didn't have long to wait. Since the 1990s, southern Spain has become the destination of choice for the diaspora of cockney cabbies * fleeing the (from my point of view, entirely welcome) wave of Eastern European and African migration that has completely revitalised the building, private car hire and domestic service industries in the Thames Estuary.

---

* These are proper cockneys too, none of your rubbish. Born between Bow Legs, the authentic Spanish cockney has been transplanted from his native habitat – which occupies a range from Grays to Bromley – into a pearly facsimile which has been painstakingly recreated on the 'Costa Del Boy' by theme pub scientists from throughout the Home Counties.

The result is a Mediterranean coastline pockmarked with English pubs, traditional fry-ups and authentic flamenco bars offering clapped-out end of the pier turns to the expatriate market. It's exactly what you might leave Britain to avoid. Unless your idea of a good time involves sitting in the middle of a vast building site while a red-faced Essex boy sells you a flyblown bacon sandwich and a slightly thinner-than-average copy of the *Daily Express* while he complains to anyone who will listen about the rising price of cabañas and all the bloody foreigners in Malaga, the Costa Del Sol is another one to cross off your list.

Search warrant: What 'coming in to water the plants' really means

If you're a homeowner, your house is probably the most expensive thing you'll ever buy. Even if you're just renting, the deposit you paid probably represents something like a month's wages. Nevertheless, there's a high probability that, before you go on holiday, you will hand the keys to that very expensive thing over to a neighbour so that they can come in and care for houseplants, fish, cats or any other living creatures that you have chosen to imprison in your home.

Let's have a think about your neighbours for a minute. What do you *really* know about them? You're probably in roughly the same income bracket, but apart from that, what do you have in common? Setting simple geography aside for now, there is one thing, and one thing alone: the natural curiosity shared by all humanity. It's our innate nosiness that make soaps and reality TV the most-watched shows on television, and made NASA spend billions for two men to play golf on the moon. Mankind's inquisitiveness has led us to the stars, and that same inquisitiveness will surely lead your neighbour to your bedside cabinet.

We've discussed elsewhere how there are some things you just can't take on holiday: certain items of underwear and other erotic accessories that are nothing to be ashamed of, but, still, you'd prefer not to think of that rather dull chap from next door chuckling in a somewhat judgemental manner. After all, how do you think the current rash of celebrity sex videos has made its way on to the Internet? Placed there by unscrupulous PRs desperate to get some notoriety for their clients? The very idea! Paris Hilton, Pamela Anderson and Abi Titmuss clearly all made the same mistake and asked the old dear in the ground floor flat to pop up and water their rubber plant. If you doubt me, just try leaving a decent bottle of wine and some cheese in your refrigerator before you go away. When you get back it will have been thoughtfully removed by a concerned citizen 'in case it went off'.

If you're a particularly private person, it's probably best to factor in the cost of new plants, cats, etc., into the price of your holiday. The rest of us should, I suppose, console ourselves with the thought that, a couple of weeks after we get back, the tables will be turned, and it will be us that hold the keys. Revenge is a dish best served cold. From someone else's fridge.

Excess baggage #1: How worry can help you shift that holiday weight

You will probably only notice it when you try to wedge yourself into your narrow economy seat for the return flight, but holidays tend to do terrible things to your weight*. Unless you are one of the fortunate minority who acquire some sort of food poisoning or voracious internal parasite while away, you will almost certainly gain a few pounds on holiday. It's not because you were greedy. Oh no. It's because, without all the usual things to

---

* It's not *all* bad news: running back up the stairs just before setting off to find a forgotten passport, again to retrieve your keys and *again* to retrieve your money only to leave the house before you remember that your tickets are on the kitchen worktop will most probably burn off a pound or two.

use to distract ourselves (like working, watching the telly, having arguments, etc.), there was nothing else to do but eat and drink. Also, foreign holidays tend to feature exotic foodstuffs with which we are unfamiliar, therefore making it more difficult to estimate the calorific content of any meal. Unlike the other sections in this book, in which I exhort you not to make the holiday mistake in the first place, I am, and I think you will agree this is to my credit, going to adopt a more understanding tone here. You've already been on holiday – now how do we put it right?

The most common approach is the fad diet. These are all centred around the idea of eating one particular food-stuff, like (for example) cabbage soup, pineapple or lard. Of course, none of these foods have any 'magic' properties. These diets rely on the fact that, by concentrating so much on the food you eat, it becomes rather unappetising, and also that too much of anything tends to get rather dull.

You could also try the alternative approach, often espoused by television companies, of having a wizened little lady coming round your house, shouting at you and smelling your poo. Well, that would be enough to put anyone off their supper, wouldn't it? Combine that with a high-fibre diet, which requires hours and hours of exhaustingly aerobic preparation for every meal, chopping up bloody artichokes, and you simply won't have the energy to eat.

There is another way, though. One that involves nei-ther alienating your neighbours with the vile stench of boiling cabbage nor the public ignominy of your excreta being displayed in Tupperware on national television: the anxiety diet.

Put simply, you can fret yourself thinner just by thinking about the right things. The best time to start is just after you've read the laminate showing people sliding out of the plane on the fun-looking bouncy castle things and before the stern-looking steward brings that volcanically hot container containing something that might once have been chicken. The beauty of my method, though, is that you can start at any time, and you can do it anywhere. *Was* that just turbulence? Or has a wing fallen off? Did you lock the front door? Did you put your email 'out of office' message on? And, *of course*, there will have been record high temperatures at home and everyone will be *loads* browner than you, making you feel like a complete fool for spending the price of a nice new telly on a pointless holiday. If you haven't lost at least a couple of ounces reading that let me know: I'll come round your house with a Tupperware container and we'll try it the traditional way.

The Samsonite Paradox: Why you can never get everything back in the case

fig.1:

Outgoing voyage luggage volume = Your stuff

fig.2:

$$\frac{\text{Return voyage luggage volume} =}{\text{Volume of stuff} + \text{volume of dirt} (\times \text{ amount of postcards you bought but didn't send})}$$

$$\overline{\text{Bulk of wine bottles that will break on the way home anyway} \div \text{complimentary robe}}$$

This apparently baffling effect can be simply explained by comparison of these two formulae: Fig.1 shows the comparatively simple mathematics of putting freshly laundered clothes into a suitcase with nothing else; Fig.2 demonstrates the effect of adding perspiration, dust, etc. to the garments* and the addition of some stolen hotel dressing gowns and a nice bottle of olive oil for the people from next door who have been looking after your plants. An explanation is not a remedy, however, and you will still end up spending most of the last day stuffing dirty socks into your pockets in an attempt to fit everything in.

* After all, only a gold-plated weirdo packs, or even looks at, a travel iron and, without one of those, there's no point in washing anything, not really. And, besides, how clean can you get your socks in a hotel sink when you're in a hurry to get out and read thick paperbacks on the beach?

7 evil things in the sea

These are only seven of hundreds, if not thousands, of aquatic horrors. Barracudas, moray eels, floating condoms and sea snakes could easily have made this list if only I could have found out some droll, yet somewhat chilling facts about them in ten minutes on the Internet. Like all of the following creatures, though, they have two characteristics in common: they are all, in their different ways, dangerous to know, and none of them live (unless you count certain carefully regulated aquaria) in British cities. I believe that the inference is clear.

The Stonefish Around a foot long and effectively invisible, the stonefish looks – as its name suggests – exactly like a stone. A stone that's bristling with spines capable of dispensing one of the world's deadliest and most painful poisons. It lives in warm shallow waters: the kind of waters, indeed, where one might be tempted to wade. If you've read this handy guide before wading, you might consider taking some precautions. Assuming you can endure the ignominy, you could, of course, buy some flip-flops or those special kind of funny-looking trainers that surfers tend to affect. A futile gesture, if you're trying to avoid the agonising death that awaits those unfortunates that step on a stonefish. For reasons that only Terry Nutkins knows for sure, the stonefish has evolved spines capable of punching through all but the thickest soles. Your choices, then, (if you are considering a coastal holiday in India, Australia or almost anywhere in the Southern Pacific) are limited to swimming in platform boots, or not going altogether. It's probably best *not* to be mistaken for Gary Glitter in South-East Asia, however so the platforms are out. And so is the holday.

The Blue-Ringed Octopus It's hard to see how the little Blue-Ringed Octopus could be particularly dangerous when the young are around the size of a pea (not even a marrowfat one, one of those little garden jobs) and, even full-grown, they are rarely bigger than a golf ball. Indeed, the bite of our little blue-ringed pal is entirely painless. You might not even notice it happen. Unfortunately, the painlessness of the bite is a result of the powerful neurotoxin secreted by the little eight-legged rascal's jaws, which effectively switches off your nervous system within a few minutes. Death is almost certain. Apparently, according to my research, nausea may also ensue. Another one from Australia, by the way. Japan too. Shame, I almost fancied Japan.

Sponges How dangerous could a sponge be? Fairly. Only about a dozen species of sponge are poisonous, but as they all look more or less the same (sort of spongey, if you haven't bought the illustrated edition) and, although some of the more dangerous ones have been given helpful names like The Red Fire Sponge (*Tedania ignis*) and the

Touch-Me-Not (*Neofibularia nolitangere*), few sponges in the wild are correctly labelled. If in doubt, please do not touch *any* sponges. The ones in Halfords might be all right, though.

The Crocodile At last! One you've heard of! Although it is possible to use crocodiles as stepping stones to cross a river, and thus avoid ruining one's safari suit, this kind of thing is best left to qualified stuntmen. The crocodile, and his (let's face it) more or less indistinguishable relatives, the alligator and the caiman, is aggressive, highly territorial and a *lot* faster on land than you would imagine. All of them would like nothing more than to drag you to the bottom of the nearest river (or estuary, depending on whether we're dealing with salt water or fresh water variants), drown you and then eat you. I accept that these are strictly river rather than sea creatures, but imagine the outcry if I hadn't mentioned them and then you went to Florida or somewhere and got dismembered.

Sea Lions Evolution is a curious thing. It's relatively easy to see how a prehistoric monkey sort-of-thing learned to swim, changed its mind and ultimately became the kind of land-based talking primate that would land on the moon and knock out mildly amusing travel books. It's less easy to understand why something that probably looked a bit like a cross between a Labrador and an otter took to the sea and ended up looking not unlike John Prescott, but that is the sea lion's journey.

Given our common mammalian heritage, you might imagine that we would get on rather well with our sea lion cousins, but, in truth, they are surly, rather territorial coves who represent more of a danger to divers than, for example, sharks do*. Especially, I'm told, during the mating season – June or July, in the case of British sea lions. The only two months, indeed, when it might be remotely tolerable to swim in otherwise frigid British waters. Tremendous.

Sharks! Really big ones! After the colossal success of *Jaws* and its decreasingly impressive sequels, there was a concerted effort by some allegedly brainy people on the radio to convince us that sharks weren't as dangerous as all that. Piffle, of course. Any shark worth his salt can smell blood from miles away and you're absolutely full of it. It would be instructive to find out where one of these shark apologists lived and pop a great white in his bath. I put it to you that our sharkophile might be a touch pungent after a week or so.

* See below. Or above, depending on whether you're the type of person that reads the whole page first, then the footnotes, or someone who skips to the footnotes first, on the off-chance that they're actually illuminating in some way. Anyway, my point is that I haven't forgotten sharks and I'm just about to get to them. Or I've just got to them, depending on your perspective. Personally, I always read the whole page, and realise that there's a footnote and have to trawl through the whole page looking for the asterisk. If that's what you've just done, it's up there in the sea lion bit. Hope that helps.

The Chironex Not, as you may have been led to believe, a poisonously bad fantasy paperback – the Chironex is a rather attractive-looking jellyfish, which, despite considerable competition, is thought to be the *most* poisonous sea creature. If one were unlucky enough to encounter one of these little chaps, you will find that he will promptly inject you with a surprisingly potent toxin. This toxin will be promptly absorbed into the bloodstream and liberally distributed around your body, causing no end of mayhem and upset. The pain is, I am reliably assured, unbearable; the tentacles are sticky and tend to adhere tightly to the skin. It would be unpleasant enough to have bits of sticky jellyfish stuck to you and (adding insult to injury) injecting more poison into your skin, but any attempt to remove them while they are still active may exacerbate the whole affair and leave quite a mark. So then, in summation: the Chironex – one to avoid. Another incredibly venomous sea creature native to Indo-Pacific and Australian waters. It's almost like someone's trying to send you a message, isn't it?

So there you have it. Seven reasons to stay ashore. It would be bad enough getting in the sea anyway, what with it being so dreadfully *wet* for one thing, and more or less engorged with sewage and johnnies, but now we find that all the animals that live in the sea seem to have taken a marked dislike to us and want to eat us, roll on us or in some way poison us. Ghastly. You may have been told that no place in the British Isles is more than 70 miles from the sea. Not half far enough, I say.

Self catering #1: What foreign supermarkets do to your mind

Unlike Britain, everyone else in the world seems to suffer from something of an embarrassment of spare room. So much so, in fact, that they can afford to build hundreds of colossal supermarkets that make that Asda Ultrastore up by the industrial estate look like a little cigarette kiosk. Of course, once they've built these great temples of Mammon, there aren't enough food products on earth to fill them, so they pack them out indiscriminately with any other products they can find: aisle after aisle of shoes, cars, electrical goods and toys are scattered (apparently) artlessly among the really confusing veg and inedible meat products. God help you if you go to one of these places with kids. You'll go in looking for some milk and maybe something for a barbecue on the last night, be browbeaten into buying a life-size inflatable alligator before you've even found the beer, end up swapping that for a 'Barbie Electronic Kitchen and War Room' that uses old Cold War computer components to randomly create delicious borscht recipes, and manage to ditch that only to come out with a ride-along animatronic dinosaur that answers your email rather tersely in Hungarian*.

Not so bad, you might think, but of course your two problems are that, first of all, you'll be so lulled by the insanely low pricing of certain items (€2.20 for a pallet of Lithuanian beer the size of a Nissan Micra? That's only about a couple of quid, isn't it? Sign me up!) that your ability to grasp the exchange rate, or even to understand the cryptic scrawl on the price tags, is lost by the second time you pass down the flannels, talc and ammunition aisle. Secondly, that the nice people at Ryanair will laugh uproariously when you pitch up at check-in with a two-metre-wide plasma TV that only receives the Pravda channel before explaining gently that every gramme of weight over the initial baggage allowance, including any weight you may have gained yourself during the holiday (either through gluttony or poor hygiene) is multiplied by a number they just thought of, rounded up to the nearest zloty, converted back into pounds and then popped over into euros, just to make it interesting, before being added on to the price of your return ticket. Terms and conditions apply. Your home may be at risk if you leave Greek refrigerators connected to the electricity supply while you sleep.

* You will, of course, be abandoning any unwanted items in randomly selected aisles rather than face the ten-minute walk back to where you found them. This converts the entire building into a sort of consumer-goods minefield for the next unlucky parent with a bored and overtired toddler along your route.

Self catering #2: What foreign food does to your soul

It is a measure of our success as a nation that, in the UK, you can buy vegetables as 'things'. A head of broccoli in a UK supermarket is washed, trimmed and contained within a hygienic plastic meniscus that pops satisfyingly for the inquisitive fingernail. Similarly, mange tout look like something you could safely eat all of without risking a mouthful of bugs, worms and dung. Not so overseas, where vegetable matter is routinely sold in great bins that are lined with the Transylvanian earth in which it must rest by day. To compound the potential problem, everything must be weighed and priced using an unfamiliar system for which few British adults have been adequately prepared. Only career drug dealers can shift between metric and imperial weights and measures with the rapidity and precision required.

It's simpler by far not to bother with veg* when that really big bag of potato crisps on the next shelf is just as plausibly your 'way to five', even if it is loaded with enough olive

* And don't even *consider* any of your woolly liberal Nestlé boycotts. In any European hypermarket you will find that, despite the apparently colossal choice on offer, the shadowy Swiss corporation manufactures everything from the mineral water to the shopping trolleys. Honestly. You thought the *Da Vinci Code* was a bit of a worry? The Milky Bar Kid is twice as bad.

oil to lubricate a battleship. In fact, you could probably lube up one battleship well enough to slip it inside another (slightly bigger) one. A fortnight-long alcohol and crisp diet will do interesting things to your digestion and, by extension, your sanity. Two weeks without a conventional bowel movement will change the way you think about yourself forever. Of course you *might* find a nice little health food shop, but, equally, you might not. Is it worth the risk?

TRAVEL TIPS #3:
EUROPE – How to ignore a Spaniard's motorbike

The outmoded and comically macho culture of Spain, so eloquently expressed in ostentatious tobacco consumption and liver-punishing alcoholic excess, reaches its apogee in the use of motorbikes and scooters. Conventional motorcyclists' clothing is eschewed, the better to exhibit the rider's tattoos, and, instead of a helmet, head protection is generally entrusted to a generously pomaded mullet. The inadequate protection afforded to the rider, though, starts to look like a suit of armour when compared to the bikini and unbuckled helmet* combo invariably chosen by his

* Ceded to the distaff motorcyclist in a display of the old world chivalry for which the Spaniard is justifiably famous.

deliciously lissom and perilously tanned pillion passenger. In fact, the skin-shredding spills that one would think were just *waiting* to happen are relatively rare. Disappointingly so, when you consider the following:

Essentially the same machines as are sold in the UK, Spanish scooters have, by law, their silencers disabled at the retailers. This modification – generally achieved by hosing the engine down with a nail gun – is what gives the Spanish scooter its devastating power. The roar of the engine, amplified by the narrow streets of the White Towns, cheers and comforts the average Spaniard by reminding him of the Falangist Stukas of his youth.

This is all very well, but for the British tourist – or for one of the legion of Essex taxi drivers who are currently in the process of replacing the indigenous Spaniards – the noise is near intolerable. Given that the fierce Iberian sun precludes the closing of any window between the months of March and October, you are left with only three defences against the sonic assault.

1: Anaesthetise oneself with cheap Spanish wine. A popular choice, limited in its effect only by the scope of one's travel insurance. As long as you're covered for cirrhosis, it's an option.

2: String piano wire across the narrow streets. High in entertainment value, but frowned upon by at least one of the several police forces that patrol the peninsula scouting for bribes. Possible, but potentially pricey.

3: (And this is my favourite) Remain in the British Isles, far from the source of the irritation. Trust me, this one's a winner.

THINGS YOU CAN ONLY DO @ HOME #3:
Comfy trousers

Everybody has a pair of Sunday trousers. Until about age thirty, both sexes tend to favour some sporty tracksuit bottoms, even though the only sport that these particular examples would be appropriate for is competitive eating. Once we reach child-bearing age, gender preference in Sunday trouser becomes more evident, with expectant fathers plumping for something in fustian to suggest stability, while their spouses stay with the trackies but upgrade to velour for that '1990s Primrose Hill Set' look. After all, you never know when Meg and Sadie are going to pop round in their Britpop Tardis, so you want to look your best when you're slumped on your sofa watching an episode of *The OC* that you've already seen at least twice but you're too overwhelmed by the baffling proliferation of Channel 4 channels to try switching over.

Comfy trousers really come into their own after a big night out. On those fuzzy Saturday mornings after a leaving party that you know you shouldn't have gone to, but it was Sam leaving and if there was ever a time for a drunken lunge it was the last night you'd ever see them and so why not, and then the next thing you know it's 2 a.m. and everybody else is ordering more cocktails, but they aren't the people you started with and you can't quite remember *how* you got home, so there really is no other trouser to wear.

So when you go on holiday, and it's one Friday night after another, why don't you pack them? Because no one does. You'll take shorts, and something nice for an evening meal, and something humiliating for the beach. That's it. No room in there for a recuperative couple of hours on the sofa. You probably won't even *have* a sofa, just a bed made with funny covers that's too close to the telly anyway. Besides, there's all that *stuff* to see: culture and buildings and such. There's no time for rest when you're on holiday. That'll have to wait until you get home and get your trackies on.

Why you can't get a saveloy in Wales

Very few people know what goes into a saveloy. Of those that do, fully 99 per cent wish they didn't. If you're not from England and you're reading this, first of all, I and all the other readers of this volume applaud you and, second of all, I'd better explain what a saveloy is:

A saveloy is a sort of spicy pork sausage, mainly red in colour, that's analogous to a black pudding. The key difference is that, whereas a black pudding is made principally of congealed blood, a saveloy is composed principally of brains. They both sound delicious, don't they? Basically, if zombies ate sausages, they'd plump for a sav every time.

Surprisingly, very few people outside southern England eat these things at all. Northerners tend, in the main, to plump for black pudding, and, of course, in Scotland, the natives feel obliged to eat haggis – no matter how vile it may taste – because they've all seen *Braveheart* and think that they probably ought.

Wales, though. Wales is a fish of an entirely different kettle. The Welshman professes, at least in public, a vegetarian diet of leeks and such. You wouldn't want to go to any country that offered vegetable broth as its chief culinary delight, now would you? To be entirely fair, a proper Welsh leek broth does contain a small amount of bacon, as even vegetarians have their limits. No one can resist bacon.

If you go into a Welsh chip shop and demand cod and chips with an English accent * the owner will, reluctantly, serve you with a cod-like fish and a crushed fistful of cold,

---

* This is you that's got the English accent. The cod is just about extinct, for a start, and, besides, even when the species was a going concern, a cod had about as much chance of pulling off a convincing English accent as Madonna.

soggy chips. Any request for a nutritious brain sausage to flesh out the meal will be met with feigned incomprehension and a derisory offer involving parsley. The Welshman, in the main, cares neither for outsiders nor for sausages of questionable provenance.

In summation, if you go to Wales expecting anything better than a disappointing soup and a burnt cottage, you're on a hiding to nothing. After all, Tom Jones is as Welsh as they come and he lives in Los Angeles, where, for all the earthquakes, riots and self-help books, you can at least get a decent fish supper.

Regrets, I've had a few: Bikinis for the over-30s

Blame Isaac Newton. Or perhaps Coco Chanel. Certainly gravity and suntanning make uneasy bedfellows: one is deliberate exposure to radiation intended to lend your epidermis an illusory glow of health in order to minimise the unappealing effect of skin which is normally not only the texture but also the colour of cottage cheese*, the other

---

* What *is* it with the weight loss industry and cottage cheese? Either they're telling you that you look like it or they're telling you that you have to eat it. It's ghastly stuff and I think we can all agree that we'd prefer it not to be mentioned again in any context. Pineapple or no pineapple.

is an insidious force that seems to exist purely for the purpose of collating all your most attractive features in one handy location, somewhere in the vicinity of your knees. Oh yes, and binding the universe together.

But which one can we do *without*? Every year a very large number of (mainly) women across the (Western) world wedge a little two-piece into a corner of their suitcase, repeating the (traditional) mantra: 'Of course, I'll never wear it.' And every year a very small number of (mainly) men continue the anti-gravity research of celebrated scientific nutcases like Thomas Townsend Brown or Kowsky and Frost. It's hard to say which is the more misguided.

It's one of those evil dichotomies that typify the whole holiday business: you're somewhere new, they've got interesting food, strangers are offering to cook it for you. You've got a lot of free time on your hands and there's nothing much to do but eat, at the same time, you're being encourage to wander around in public wearing not much more than your bra and pants, like some loser who's forgotten their gym kit. All the time, gravity is working, day and bloody night, pulling bits of you that were in the right place into unauthorised locations. It just won't do, will it?

Clearly, something has to change. Either we learn to nullify gravity, which may lead to the collapse of the entire cosmos and the end of time as we understand it, or we forget about going a bit brown next summer. It's hard to decide, but it's certainly something to think about.

5 quite ghastly exotic diseases and where to get them

Most deaths in temperate urban environments like our own are directly attributable to our uniquely comfortable lifestyle. We either die from having too much butter in our sandwiches, or a surfeit of cigars, or from having too splendid an automobile. Venture too far, though, from a broad ellipse bounded by New York on the left-hand side and Berlin over to the right and you find yourself in a purgatory of vile infestations that make the greater part of our planet uninhabitable for all right-thinking people. Indeed, the vast numbers of eminently sensible people that are doing all they can to move from these other, warmer parts of the world to our little enclave of temperate loveliness are in themselves a persuasive proof of the theory that much of the earth, and especially the tropical section, just isn't worth bothering with at all. You've probably heard of all the big hits, like malaria, tuberculosis and Ebola, but here are a few more comparatively little-known conditions that are out there waiting for the intrepid traveller.

Hantavirus Pulmonary Syndrome There's more to Florida than Disney, overfed British tourists and electoral irregularities. Hantavirus Pulmonary Syndrome is a respiratory ailment spread by rats and mice in inadequately cleaned kitchens. The kind of kitchens that might possibly cater to a near-endless stream of families that have spent most of their holiday money on Disney Princess tat and are looking to eke out their budget at least until the end of the first week. Few diseases could be described as nice, but this one's especially nasty. It's caused by the Sin Nombre virus. A quick riffle though that Spanish dictionary you quixotically bought (but forgot to pack) before last year's rain-marred week in Alicante will tell you that what we're talking about is a Virus With No Name. You won't care what it's called if you catch it. After a week or so of what seems like a nasty cold, you'll take a turn for the worse and effectively drown in your own blood. Still, a pair of wrecked lungs is a rather more individual souvenir than a Mickey Mouse sweatshirt you could easily have bought in the Arndale Centre.

Leishmaniasis   Leishmaniasis is quite widespread across most of the popular long-haul destinations but is most prevalent in the 'gap year triangle' of India, Bangladesh and Nepal. It's a fairly standard 'blood-sucking insect is sick into your veins giving rise to a vast colony of parasitic organisms in your guts' type of ailment that you will find pretty much anywhere that's warmer then Surrey. If you're lucky, it just sets up camp in your skin, giving rise to leprous-looking scarring and profound discomfort. Less fortunate souls will contract the visceral variant of Leishmaniasis, which wasn't treatable for most of mankind's history, then briefly was, and is now evolving a resistance to pretty much everything we can throw at it and should be more or less invulnerable to all known medicines by the middle of next summer. Visceral Leishmaniasis kills rather more than half a million people a year but because it's endemic to the Sudan region, which has been at war continuously since the end of the progressive rock era, it's becoming significantly more widespread as refugees from that area quite sensibly migrate further afield in search of some peace and bloody quiet.

Myiasis   Myiasis is just too nasty to discuss*, really. Let's just say that it's caused by three different species of flies living in a wide range from Southern Europe to Australia. And it's horrible.

Lymphatic Filariasis   Again with the mosquitoes. This time they're teaming up with worms to parasitise your lymphatic system, leading to (in the first instance) the feelings of general lassitude one might reasonably expect to have after a solid fortnight of unstinting devotion to spicy food and refreshing local lagers. Once the first wave of worms die in your lymph nodes, however, you can expect grossly distended legs, unsightly

---

* Not only unpleasant to discuss, but unpleasant (let me assure you) to research. If you find yourself typing 'Myiasis' into Google just to see what all the fuss is about, do not, I implore you, look at the example video. There are maggots.

bulges in the groin and general all-round elephantiasis. Which is nasty. Egypt may entice with its pyramids and sphinxes and so on, but the real curse of the pharaohs is this horrible, debilitating and disfiguring disease. You probably won't die of Lymphatic Filariasis, but if you catch it, you might find yourself wishing from time to time that you would.

Chagas Disease Pretty much all of the tropics is overrun with irritating insects of one stripe or another. It's almost as if someone is telling us that we should confine ourselves to the nicer parts of the planet and leave the rest of it to the six-legged fraternity. To enforce this notion, many insects practise a type of biological warfare, wherein they carry around unpleasant microscopic organisms seemingly for the express purpose of introducing them into our bloodstreams so that they might cause some manner of minuscule mayhem. Chagas Disease is one more example of this vile policy. Its most famous victim is Charles Darwin, who, not knowing when he was on to a good thing, left the entirely pleasant environs of Shropshire in order to gad about the Galapagos pestering tortoises. En route he contracted a dose of Chagas for his trouble, which enfeebled him to such an extent that he was more or less confined to his bed for the last fifty years of his life. An entirely agreeable fate, one might think, but one that he could have selected for himself without ever leaving the perfectly pleasant market town in which he was born. You may have heard about how 'awesome' and 'incredible' Machu Picchu is, but I bet Chagas wasn't in the brochure.

TRAVEL TIPS #4:
EUROPE – How to cope with a French dog

It will come as no surprise, I am sure, when I tell you that the British attitude to dogs (and, furthermore, to pets in general) is more or less unique. Simple givens like clearing up after your dog, for example, are unheard of in France. Indeed, in summer months, the pavements of Nice are so thickly carpeted with dog turds that they are effectively covered in a rather attractive poo parquet. Impressionable German tourists are occasionally overheard muttering bitterly that you can't get anything like it in their local B und Q.

If it were simply the need to be extra-cautious when wearing sandals, though, the French canine would be no more inimical to one's well-being than, say, a benefit fraudster's standard-issue pitbull-cross. No, the real issue we need to concern ourselves with here is the likelihood, nay the certainty, that any French dog will be infected with rabies. Our island is well-provisioned with defences against this terrible disease in the shape of a twenty-mile-wide body of water and a sign at the mouth of the Channel

Tunnel asking any stray dogs or foxes to just hang around at the entrance like a good chap until someone pops along to give them the old once-over, so it is generally on holiday that the issue first arises.

The urban French dog, available in a smallish Poodle configuration that seems to have been bred expressly for the purpose of cleaning the inside of Thermos flasks with its tail, is, of course, a mere bagatelle to the doughty British tourist, who will flick it aside with the toe of a well-polished brogue. The real problem arises when travelling in the French countryside, where one might meet the second, and more dangerous, breed of French dog: the Non-Specific Yellow. These animals are like Lord Byron, not so much in their ability to knock out a catchy ode (although that has been, on some rare occasions, known) as in the undeniable fact that they are, to a dog, mad, bad and *extremely* dangerous to know. On encountering the paler type of person, they will attempt to back them into a corner and bark loudly in French until that person is at least thoroughly intimidated if not leaking a quantity of blood from some valued extremity.

My dear mother once advised me, if confronted by an angry dog, to thrust my fist between its jaws – a tactic that would theoretically negate its power to deliver a potentially fatal bite. In hindsight, this approach is not always the most advisable, because it fails to take into account any disparities of scale that the smaller person's fist might have with regard to the jaw-span of the larger dog. I would be happy to show the more doubtful reader, on request, a pair of matching houndstooth scars on the back of my hand and my palm if it will serve to dissuade them from this erroneous course of action.

The only foolproof approach, of course, is to remain out of the extensive natural range of the Non-Specific Yellow (and his slavering jaws), which begins, like so many unpleasant things, at Calais.

Sand: Everybody's favourite kind of dirt

One of the standard photographic tropes of softcore pornography is the well-turned buttock with a fine coating of sand. Now, that's all well and good. We accept that the Internet is a special place. They do things differently there. It's certainly warmer, for a start. It must be: the people on the Internet wear a *lot* less clothing.

Imagine, though, for a minute, that the lithe young model in the picture was wearing a thin layer of mud. All of a sudden you're in a special interest group. People will be asking for your credit card number. You might even be invited to sign some sort of register.

But that's what sand really is: dirt. Some people want you to believe that it's somehow special. They lie about on it. They use it to create little imaginary buildings and sometimes quite elaborate trench systems for the amusement of their offspring. After a day's occupation by holidaymakers, the average beach resembles the aftermath of El Alamein. Like Rommel and Montgomery competing to claim the greatest amount of wasteland, beach enthusiasts even buy little paper flags* representing the component parts of the British Isles to stick in the sand. Flags or no flags, it's still dirt.

Scientifically, the only way to distinguish between sand and dirt is to establish whether you are statistically more likely to find a spider or a crab on it. I don't know about you, but if I'm planning on lying on any surface for a period of time, I'd prefer to find neither. You can even make a pile of dirt into a pile of sand by the simple addition of a measured quantity of cigarette ends. It's been done: I invite you to gaze upon Soho Square at the very centre of our nation's proud capital. Once a grassy quadrangle of fertile soil, it has been transformed into a sterile and sandy wasteland by generation after generation of nicotine-crazed lunch-hour picnickers. So it is with the beaches of the world. The only quality they have to boast about is an inability to host vegetation. It's hardly a recommendation, is it?

* The flags are, it has to be admitted, great, though. There's a little harp one, which is probably Ireland or somewhere, a dragon – that's likely to be Wales or maybe China. The three lions one, that's Skinner and Baddiel. Their country's called Avalon, I think.

Where do I look? An Englishman's guide to the topless beach

It is our misfortune to live in an age of flux. (Say what you like about the Chinese, they know how to make up a top quality curse.) The female breast is still technically a taboo area in our culture, even though images of it routinely appear in popular daily newspapers. What those images are doing there is anybody's guess: neither strictly news nor honest smut, Page Three is one of those things we've all agreed to ignore in the interests of a quiet life. Clearly, a change is afoot. And nowhere is this change more apparent than on holiday beaches. Nudists were once (quite justifiably, in my view) confined to camps where they could be carefully monitored and documented in newsreels and specialist magazines. No wonder so many Germans took it up. Yet, at some point in the late 1970s, when Britain was at its lowest ebb, standards began to slip. First of all on the Continent, as one might expect, but then at home, until, on warmer days, even our great metropolitan parks might play host to young women keen to acquire a melanoma on or near the nipple. Now it is rare to find any strip of land where the surf meets the dirt that is not sullied by at least a certain degree of untoward bosom exposure.

For the heterosexual gentleman at least, this is something of a puzzler. Breasts displayed in such circumstances, and in such bewildering variety, may well lose a certain amount of their erotic appeal, but their ability to fascinate remains undimmed. The true multiplicity of possible cup sizes, skewed in our minds by the ubiquity of Jordan in the popular media, becomes mesmerisingly apparent. Even the gayest caballero might take a passing interest in the bounties displayed. For the fairer sex, too, the opportunity to compare their own blessings with the unpadded gifts of potential rivals is often difficult to resist. And yet we are frequently looked upon askance if we allow our perfectly natural interest to flower into a full-bodied stare.

And rightly so! These taboos were put in place by our arboreal forefathers for a perfectly good reason. To openly stare is considered, amongst all primates, tantamount to a declaration of war. To those species unable to transmit telegrams, it remains the only universally accepted declaration of martial intent. Indeed, even among humans, the stare is still employed for that purpose in football stadia and licensed premises throughout the land. It is not something to be done lightly.

Similarly, the comparative uniqueness of the human female breast (unless you're going to get all weird about dugongs and manatees and, if you are, frankly, the rest of us would prefer it if you left) lends the entire affair an air of fruitiness that is criminally devalued by overexposure. Bosoms should be kept in their place (with stiff and uncomfortable wires, if necessary), which is, as we all accept, on the Internet and very occasionally in a coy Rankin photoshoot for a gentleman's interest magazine.

Until this uncertain situation is resolved, either with the restoration of a perfectly good taboo or its regrettable abandonment, beaches and, indeed, many other open spaces, are best avoided.

Mini-bars: Overpriced, understocked and over there

It's too hot to sleep, and you find yourself mixing a miniature of Bacardi into a tin of Fanta Lemon that alone costs more than an eminently quaffable bottle of Jacob's Creek would in your local offie. That's when you know you've hit bottom. It's time to come home.

Caravans explained

British architecture is acknowledged as some of the ugliest in the known world. Every architect trained in these fair isles feels obliged, at some point in his (or her, although not as often) career, to draw up at least one utterly repugnant neo-brutalist concrete turd in tribute to his imaginary Soviet masters. Nevertheless, the buildings of Britain have one shared virtue that lifts them into the realm of the tolerable: they are not on wheels. By contrast the caravan is a distressing invention that combines the pleasing odour of a rock festival Portaloo with the stability of a crack-addled rollerblader. Or is it the other way around?

Caravans are for people who are cheap enough to consider a camping holiday, but feel that life under canvas lacks the white-knuckle thrills of a motorway pile-up and would like, consequently, to factor that additional hazard into the equation*. Many caravans are, of course, kept permanently in one location, substantially obviating the necessity of wheels and rather begging the question: 'Why didn't you just buy a nice shed from the back of the *Radio Times* instead?' Please don't ask any caravan people that question, though. I tried, and was rewarded with a rather hard stare.

I didn't really expect much of an answer, mind you – caravanning is a strange quasi-Masonic world, with its own magazines, secret handshakes and uniform of beige windbreakers. There's probably a novel exposing its dark secrets called *The Romany Conspiracy*, or *The Highway Code*, or something like that. You're not reading that now, though, so don't expect any more revelations about the

---

* Or, equally, the kind of oddball that thinks that hearing a close relative thunderously urinating into a bucket through a thin partition wall is the kind of thing that brings a family together.

shadowy world of practical caravanners from me. All you need to know is that caravans always smell of warm Weetabix and wee, and that you really don't want to find yourself in one at any cost.

Signal and points failures explained. Eventually

Trains may be the more eco-friendly way to travel, but they can also be unbearably stressful. If you've ever woken from a pleasant post-work nap, looked out of the train window and not been entirely sure where you were for a moment, multiply that feeling of mild discombobulation by about 1138 per cent to approximate the sheer visceral panic of realising that Vilnius isn't just a quaintly idiomatic spelling of Vienna and that, far from a pleasant weekend in waltz country, you're on the overnight express to the Arctic Circle. It's one thing gaily whipping your laptop off the luggage rack and getting a £20 minicab home, altogether another manhandling a suitcase the size of a coffin up a narrow train corridor and explaining to the Slovakian-speaking conductor that it's an honest mistake that you got on the wrong train, so a night in the Bratislava police cells might not be the best thing for you at all.

A long train journey can also be the catalyst for the realisation that you have nothing in common with your family at all: real life has numerous insulating distractions, like work, school and anaesthetising afternoons at the garden centre, to keep us from all tearing one another's throats out. Grimly staring for three hours across a narrow Formica table at someone who, while they may bear a slight resemblance to you, sniffs more frequently than is necessary and has used up all the laptop battery watching Disney Princess DVDs has brought out the feral impulse in better men than you, let me assure you.

I shan't even stoop to discuss those misguided individuals who have, one hopes as a result of some temporary stress-related condition, elected to 'Go Inter-Railing'. Setting aside for one moment the ineluctable truth that Inter-Rail is not, never has been and never will be a verb, the simple fact is that sitting on a series of poorly sprung Balkan train seats for a couple of months is not going to broaden your mind, just your fundament.

In conclusion, I would ask you to cast your mind back to your journey home from work once more. Consider, if you will, the parlous state of the UK's rail network. Ponder for a moment on the slipshod and frequently hazardous quality of maintenance work performed upon the track. Track along which, I would remind you, we could potentially hurtle at speeds of up to 125 mph. The permanently work-shy and frequently tipsy Frenchman has a train that is quite capable of rattling along his sloppily bolted-together Hornby set at a positively petrifying 356 mph. The reason that our trains are frequently delayed for apparently fanciful reasons, like 'staff shortage' or 'leaves on the line', is that that the actual truth is so unpalatably terrifying that, were it to be widely known, no sane person would ever buy a train ticket again: if the points or the signals are not working absolutely perfectly, the occupants of any train passing through them will almost certainly end up being crushed, burned or thrown hundreds of feet into a thistly embankment. Luckily for us, our rail carriers care too much about our safety to have the trains travelling at anything above walking pace, and they cancel any service that might, at any point, pass within fifty miles of a questionably maintained piece of track. Unfortunately, the casual temperament of the Continental or (God forbid) the suicidal optimism of the Indian rail traveller means that trains run at perilously high speeds, are rarely delayed and are hardly ever cancelled, placing thousands of passengers in mortal peril every day. Ask yourself: Are you willing to risk your life just to see a few bloody vineyards?

It's Chico Time! The myth of the Latin waiter

Picture the typical English lover and you're probably picturing someone like Hugh Grant: all stuttering reticence and floppy-fringed insecurity. He's a man who, whereas he's got a fair idea which team he's batting for now, fondly remembers furtive masturbation with Roberts minor behind the cricket pav. before Latin prep as one of his formative experiences. He is not a man who is especially comfortable around the opposite sex. In fact, he would probably prefer you not to mention sex at all, if at all possible. Thanks awfully.

By contrast, the Continental lothario is a man who takes Marcello Mastriano, or perhaps Alain Delon, as his model. His formative years were spent learning the best way to comb his hair, smoke a cigarette and ride a scooter, probably all at once. When they were handing out leaving certificates at his primary school, he was practising lovebites behind the bicycle sheds. Probably on his sister. This is a man who is neither circumspect nor, indeed, circumcised in his dealings with women.

Now, a certain type of Englishwoman, perhaps one who regrettably lacks a degree of self esteem, or perhaps a lady who has left behind the first bloom of youth and hasn't got so much life expectancy left that she can afford to mess about, values directness in a lover. This, in itself, is no crime. She may find herself charmed by the attentions of the swarthy *camarero* and find herself at least passingly charmed by his strongly accented flattery. One should, however, remember that the average Greek or Italian waiter, like many catering personnel throughout the known world, has not selected his career path out of a keen interest in gastronomy or a desire to serve others so much as a lack of qualifications and the desire to pick up as many chicks in a summer season as his shift pattern allows.

If all that the *tourista* desires is a brief coupling in her hotel room, and fears neither society's ill-founded censure nor genital warts, then all well and good: it's as much a part of the package holiday as sangria or sunburn. The difficulty creeps in when one allows oneself to feel a misplaced affection for the pomaded plaything and, as so often happens, to consider continuing the liaison beyond the buffet breakfast. These are, in the main, men of the Catholic persuasion, and with the concomitant conflicted regard for women.

Now, I have nothing against the Catholic church. Indeed, with its laudably hypocritical amassing of capital toward the upper echelons of the organisation, while paying lip service to illusory notions of egalitarianism and decency, it serves as the original business model for our own splendid financial system. However, Catholic societies also have an expectation of married women which generally involves staying at home, putting on a good deal of weight, preparing elaborate rice or pasta dishes and bringing up vast fleets of children while the husband plys his trade as cocktail waiter and part-time gigolo. This is more than a little at variance with our own concepts of a woman's natural career freedoms. And that's before you meet his mother. Now, you can just as easily cop off with a sexist dimwit in your own street, but at least, with the benefit of a common language and a second opinion from your dad, you have the opportunity of making some value judgements about his future worth, rather than basing your marital plans on your suitor's passing resemblance to Tom Conti after forty quid's worth of San Tropez tan.

THINGS YOU CAN ONLY DO @ HOME #4:
Drinking tap water

Blame the French. Everybody does. For everything. Especially, though, for those astoundingly expensive bottles of a substance which routinely falls from the sky and which one might, therefore, reasonably expect to get for free. Evian, Vittel, Perrier: generally packed in plastic bottles that leach poisonous antimony into their contents at a rate that would terrify any homeopath. The British, for all their self-proclaimed faults, can deliver a nice glass of water to your tap whenever you fancy it. Hosepipe bans permitting.

Shockingly, there is no potable water available on mainland Europe, or not for free, at any rate, which represents a lucrative sales opportunity for a few large drinks manufacturers. Chemically speaking, there is very little to distinguish these premium offerings from the liquid that flows from your tap*. Of course, there's probably a bit less

---

* The first reader to come out with some pseudo-scientific new-age claptrap about 'energy' or 'toxins' gets a Chinese burn.

limescale in the bottled stuff, but you could easily eliminate that by popping a couple of cubes of Calgon in your glass.

Therefore, any trip taken outside the British Isles carries with it the additional hidden expense of at least a couple of euros a day for mineral water. Not a huge sum, admittedly, but bear in mind that while you are away you will be drinking a good deal more alcohol than usual in order to stave off the boredom and marital friction; and will consequently probably be drinking more water than normal, generally in a fit of mid-morning self loathing. When you are groggily rueing the unconscionable sum you squandered on ouzo the previous night, the last thing you need is having even more cash gouged out of you by some Frenchie cashing in on mainland Europe's questionable plumbing.

The airport: Dehydrated wonderland

Unlike hotels, which at least carry some sort of illusory erotic charge (or is that just me?), airports are the most miserable places on earth. There is little jet set glamour to be had in a modern airport, which is essentially just a vast shopping mall with armed police. And no proper shops. There's an urban legend that, on her return from the United States, Sid Vicious's mum dropped his ashes on the concourse at Heathrow. Because no fresh air is allowed to enter the complex, the ashes of the misguided punk rocker are said to still circulate in the air conditioning system. It probably isn't true, but certainly the ashes of a million holiday hopes are left there every day.

Airports are where the holiday dream goes to die: the notions of freedom from work, liberation from domestic drudgery and the promise of exotic discoveries are quickly ground out of holidaymakers by delays, stale air and the atmosphere of ennui that radiates from every check-in clerk, baggage checker and shop assistant. They see people like you every day, they probably get paid half what you do and will never go to where you're going, so if they're having a crap day, they see no reason why you shouldn't share in the experience. *The Terminal*, a film which shows a man subsisting against all the odds in an inimical airport environment, was just one of four films about the same events*. This isn't because airports are intrinsically fun places to make films in; it's because that man's struggle against the harshest of environments is inspiring and terrifying in much the same way as Captain Scott's quixotic race to the South Pole, or your struggle to get though an overcomplicated sentence that (against all good sense) contains (many) (indeed very many) more parentheses that any (sane) man (or woman) could

* *Here to Where, Waiting for Godot at DeGaulle* and *Tombés du ciel* are the others, if you're planning a really dull film festival.

reasonably be expected (ever) to have to deal with. In fact, poor Merhan Nasseri, the subject of the four films, was so traumatised by the experience that he may have lost it entirely. Despite having been paid over a quarter of a million dollars for his story, he still lives in the Paris airport where he has been stranded since 1988. That's what airports do to people. Please don't let it happen to you.

What the hell is *in* this? Paella and other horrors

One of the things upon which most reasonable people find themselves broadly in agreement is apartheid. It's generally considered to be, at best, misguided and, at worst, (and it normally is worst) the work of thoroughgoing bastards. And that's just as it should be, except in one crucial area: the area (of course) of food.

The classic British meat and two veg meal is a dish where every component knows its place and keeps to it, only to be united in blissful union with its fellows in the privacy of the diner's mouth. As a people, we tend to favour plain dealing over obfuscation and this is reflected in the clarity, directness and unapologetic *blandness* of our national palate.

Yes, there are hotpots, stews and that French cuckoo in the nest, the casserole, but these are to be viewed more as excessively be-gravied meat and two veg approximations created out of exigency by the underprivileged diner rather than as part of the great conspiracy of culinary deceit that is Continental *cuisine*. Think of them, if you will, as crustless pies.

Cuisine is not the same stuff as food. Not by a long courgette. The whole point of *cuisine* is to confuse and upset the British as a sort of subtly garlic-scented revenge for Agincourt, Waterloo and Eurovision 1981. And French food is, it has to be accepted, one of the more comprehensible varieties, while the bizarre aquatic nature ramble that is paella comprises a grab-bag of beachcombers' discoveries bound together with rice that, for reasons we're too polite to discuss, has been stained the colour of a drunkard's urine.

Further afield, in hotter climes, we will encounter meats that have been steeped in strong spices, partly as a preservative to stave off the rapid putrescence one has to expect in high temperatures and partly to disguise it when it inevitably occurs. Thus are engendered chillis, curries and satays. (Not to be confused with that delicious pretend Thai food that, for some reason, is endemic to suburban British pubs.) Yes, you can sample the exciting 'street food' that other, lesser, guide books keep banging on about, but do bear in mind that the vendors of those delicacies are subject to the same financial constraints as the owners of dodgy burger vans, Mystery Fried Chicken and other classic British 'street foods' with the same concomitant economies made on ingredients, hygiene and so forth.

A vast shadowy conspiracy of marketing men and spin doctors have spent millions on popularising cuddly terms like *Delhi Belly* or *Montezuma's Revenge*, but rebranding E. coli and amœbic dysentery does not serve to make them any the less debilitating. Nietzsche memorably suggested that 'What does not kill you, makes you stronger'. What an idiot. The Germans, uniquely, have a diet even more laudably prosaic than our own, so you can see how he made his mistake, though.

Ibiza: The new Saturnalia

Spain enjoyed a reputation, throughout the late 1960s and early 1970s, as the only dictatorship in which one could take an affordable summer holiday*. With the advent of cheap mass air travel in the latter part of the 1970s, other totalitarian states, like Cuba, suddenly came into the price bracket of the common man as well. Around the same time, Generalissimo Franco was regrettably called to the great bierkeller in the sky, so

---

* Say what you like about undemocratic forms of government, but the public transport under such leadership is always terribly reliable and the streets are so clean you could eat your dinner off them. In fact, under certain unfortunate circumstances, you might be invited to. At gunpoint.

if it was to retain the profitability of its tourist economy, Spain needed an angle. Also at around the same time, Ecstasy, which had been a stable of New York's gay club culture for a number of years, began its rush to popularity, culminating in the Acid House summer of 1988.

Some bright spark within the militant wing of the provisional Spanish Tourist board spotted the connection early, and with the aid of some prurient tabloid exposés and a few compilation CDs with subliminally persuasive titles, like *Now! Drugged-up Ibiza pill house sweaty T–shirt drugs party! With drugs!*, British consumers began to suspect that there might be a better, and warmer, place to get in a major MDMA pickle than some cowpat-littered field in Berkshire.

Soon anybody who was anybody among Britain's influential media set was travelling to Ibiza to spend their whole summer up to their nipples in foam, necking Doves and dancing rather badly to a subtle blend of rigorous Detroit Techno and godawful holiday records. And where the hip young journalist from *The Spectator* or *Chat* leads, the common man inevitably follows. Hopefully bringing his wallet. The quality of music, foam and drugs have all declined since those heady early days – you're as likely to buy a half-sucked Mint Imperial as a decent pill in Manumission today – but, nevertheless, the knock-on effect has revitalised Spain's once flagging tourist industry, and, by extension, its entire economy, which is why, even today, every loyal Spaniard proudly affixes a sticker to his car, in tribute to the party drug that saved his nation, which simply says 'E'.

THINGS YOU CAN ONLY DO @ HOME #5:
Going to the pictures

No matter how many bowdlerised cuts of *Se7en* are broadcast on Living TV, or how many well-meaning Chinamen thoughtfully offer you a DVD of *Spiderman 6* out of a suitcase in the precinct, there's still no substitute for a night at the pictures. The entire experience of eating that vast skip of deliciously dehydrating popcorn and realising you really should have spent the extra £9.50 for a Fanta; watching the trailers that, regardless of the quality of the source material, are artfully cut to look like masterpieces; and finally watching two or more hours of jolly nonsense that's been filleted of any original features and then confirmed as thoroughly undemanding by dim, corn-fed Idaho preview audiences is a genuine joy. For the childless, anyway. Once you start reproducing, you tend to go to the cinema more rarely, and earlier in the day. On the upside, if we're being honest with ourselves, Pixar movies are generally rather better than Mike Leigh ones, and they're a good deal less patronising about the British working class.

Unfortunately, in a trend of directorial one-upmanship that defies all commercial good sense, films are getting longer and longer. Consequently, we have less and less time to watch the bloody things and so we end up seeing them on the television a couple of years late, with all the swearing, sex, violence and other good bits winnowed out.

So our holiday time might seem like the ideal opportunity to settle back and watch two and a half hours of delightfully sweary Tarantino nonsense. But, of course, we can't. For a start, if you watch films in other countries, they will almost invariably have been dubbed into some comically inaccessible language, like French or something. Failing that, they will have two lines of subtitles emblazoned across the very area at the bottom of the screen where one might normally hope to see the nipples of a promising young actress. Disappointing for many male cineastes, as well as a good proportion of female viewers of a certain stripe. That's assuming that you can see the screen, of course, as Moran's Law – which dictates that for every ten miles you travel away from Highgate you also go back in time one year – will mean that, for many popular holiday destinations, it's still 1947 and the air in the poorly ventilated fleapit will be so thick with tobacco smoke that you will barely be able to see your popcorn.

Furthermore, there will inevitably be some spoilsport in your party who insists on *doing* things on holiday. And most of these things seem to involve being outside looking at very old dull stuff rather than being indoors watching exciting new, if comfortingly predictable, stuff. It's always seemed suspicious to me that, although almost every part of Europe and Asia was at one point occupied by the odious Axis powers and then subsequently bombed flat by the thoroughly decent Allies, there seem to be an *implausible* number of old buildings and other assorted monuments that one is rather unreasonably required to visit. If you consider that the doughty pavements of our own land have never known the taste of the jackboot and yet you'd be hard pressed to find any building in London built before last Wednesday morning, it's clear that something mighty peculiar is going on.

So, in summation: if you like films (and everybody does a bit), then you can't possibly see them while you're at work (unless you're Jonathan Ross*), and even in the evenings they're too long to watch if you want to stand any chance of being up for work the next morning, but you can't watch them if you go abroad because they've been messed about with and they're all full of foreign. It's simple really, isn't it?

* In the unlikely event that you *are* Mr Jonathan Ross, the impressively remunerated television and radio personality, I would just like to go on record in saying that I am very fond of your work and perhaps you might consider drawing the attention of your many viewers and listeners to the notion that they might like to buy this moderately droll book. Thanks awfully. Cheerio.

City breaks, and the lure of the overdraft

I think we all accept that cities are the very best places to live. That's why so many people live in them. The trouble with that essentially laudable policy is that the competition for space has the effect of driving up prices of luxuries, like accommodation and travel, as well as the basics, like coffee and steamed milk in paper cups.

'But where does all that leave me, the jolly holidaymaker?' you might ask, if you were the kind of person who had only skim-read the preceding pages and hadn't really got a grip on what I've been trying to say.

What it means for you, the jolly holidaymaker, is this. You may be familiar with the work of Dr James Ephraim Lovelock. He is the architect of a hypothesis about our planet known to tabloid newspaper subeditors as The Gaia Theory. You haven't got time to read a full description of the thing – after all, we've already established that you've only skim-read *this* book up to now and you don't have an entirely clear idea of what I'm on about – but, in essence, Lovelock describes a self-healing system. If you plant enough dark-coloured flowers to make the earth less reflective, the climate will change and so some of the flowers will die out and you'll be back to where you started. That's enough about gardening, though, here's my point: cities, too, are essentially self-healing systems. Although they're very expensive places to inhabit, city dwellers are generally so busy working they haven't got enough free time to spend much money and, therefore, maintain a tolerable standard of solvency.

If you're on holiday, there is no such natural protection. You've got nothing to do all day but wander around expensive shopping streets buying things you don't particularly need from shops that (increasingly) are the same shops you'd have in your own home town anyway, and the only respite you'll get is the occasional very expensive paper cupful of coffee and steamed milk in a pavement café. And because you won't have been working during the day, there won't be any satisfying slump on the sofa while you watch *CSI* either. You'll have to go to an expensive bar and drink cocktails you can ill afford until it's time to go back to the hotel instead. And you won't even get a decent night's sleep in your expensive hotel either, because the room will be knee-deep with Mango and Jigsaw carrier bags. City breaks are supposed to be exciting, sexy affairs, but if you make the mistake of booking yourself on one, you'll be too oppressed by the punishing expense of it all to feel even remotely fruity.

So why would anyone select a city break holiday? It's a very good question. Compared to the privations of camping or the terrors of the tropics, a proper night's sleep in a proper city seems like the safest option. Then again, you can get a proper night's sleep at home, can't you?

Holiday photos: Why nobody wants to see them

In happier, simpler times, people would come home from their holidays with approximately thirty-six photographs. Some of them would have a sticker on pointing out that the lens cap had been left on, or that someone had their thumb over the lens. Once in a while, a budding photographer would get one of his prints back from Boots with the rare 'Too much cellulite in image' sticker – very much the Penny Black of bad photography sticker enthusiasts. Allowing for this natural wastage, the average holiday would rarely yield more than about twenty usable images. If you were unfortunate enough to visit friends or relatives in the first eleven months after their return from holiday, you might well expect to have to riffle though these 'holiday snaps' out of politeness, as the subjects grinned at you over the flap of the Prontaprint envelope, mercifully more modestly dressed than when they were photographed, but, as long as you took care not to ask any questions about what you were being shown, it would take about three precious seconds of your life for every print. Seasoned dinner party guests would develop a palming technique worthy of the great Paul Daniels, wherein they flipped two pictures at a time back into the colourful envelope, thus only viewing 50 per cent of the images of their hosts clad effectively in their underclothes depicted against the backdrop of some foreign locale distinguished only by its wealth of other lobster-red Brits in unwisely chosen swimwear.

Not so today, in the digital age: even the most modest digital camera can carry a monstrous payload of images. With a couple of spare memory cards, the undiscriminating holiday-maker can bring home thousands of photographs that mean little to them, and absolutely nothing to anyone else. And they want to show them all to you. A modest 4-megapixel camera with a one gigabyte card could easily deliver 488 images to your unwilling eyes. That's about half an hour of nodding and smiling at someone's laptop or (worse still), if they've brought home the 'old projector' from work, at a strangely out-of-register image on their front room wall that will be hauntingly reminiscent of a 1950s 3D movie *. Thirty minutes of that will give you a blinding headache that makes the aftermath of that £3.99 Asda Merlot they foisted on you seem like a fondly remembered dream.

The things is, your holiday photos may seem very interesting and, indeed, impressive to *you*, being, after all, the only tangible evidence of your punishingly expensive trip to Eilat, but for anyone who did not share in the bonding experience of a four-hour wait in the departure lounge at Haifa, they aren't quite the thrill ride you imagine.

---

* I can't *guarantee* a *Creature from The Black Lagoon*, but the likelihood exists.

Indeed, to outsiders, your holiday snaps are worse than dull, they are (candidly) an affront to the senses.

Tipping: The wrong way and the *wrong* way

It is part of the mysterious secret doctrine of hoteliers that the bags that you've hauled down your stairs, into the car, out of the car, through the Byzantine maze of airport security, on to a little bus thing and then into a taxi suddenly become too heavy for you to bear once you have dragged them as far as the hotel lobby. As a consequence, a specialist is employed to hump a couple of suitcases on to a curiously top-heavy trolley and push the thing into the lift for you. Once this comparatively simple task is achieved, the highly trained trolley pilot, known inexplicably as a bellboy despite the fact that he wears some suspiciously shiny black trousers and a vile nylon shirt rather than the Morris dancing regalia one might reasonably expect, will hang around the doorway like a bad smell until he has been given a tip.

Now, in the UK, that's just a mild annoyance. Overseas, however, it's a pain in the neck of an entirely different colour. Even after the convenient amalgamation of all European currencies into one unpopular system the money's all a bit baffling: the coins are effectively valueless tokens that hover just below foil-wrapped chocolate ones on the world currency markets, and the notes are all so absurdly similar that it's as easy to deal the bellboy a mortal insult with a comically low tip as it is to pay off his mortgage. Inadvertently gravitating to either extreme will make your holiday a miserable affair, as you either spend every waking hour exiled from the hotel for fear of encountering a vengeful bellhop or every minute of the fortnight imprisoned in your hotel room by your own lack of spending money while the hotel staff sit in the downstairs bar lighting colossal cigars with fifty euro notes at your expense.

The increased popularity of the longer-haul destinations make this dilemma even sharper: slipping a fiver into a plucky British dustman's hand at Christmas is a simple enough affair; surreptitiously palming a wheelbarrowful of effectively valueless currency to a Laotian waiter requires a preternatural deftness which would represent a challenge to a thoroughly sober David Blaine. Expecting this of an Englishman mildly anaesthetised by perilously cheap rice wine is patently unrealistic.

The alternative, of course, is to spend a couple of weeks in one of Britain's increasingly balmy suburban gardens, seated at some garden furniture which B&Q will sell you for the price of a taxi to the airport, taking turns with your companions to lash up the next jug of Pimms with no embarrassing gratuities required.

THINGS YOU CAN
ONLY DO @ HOME #6:
Dress appropriately

The weather is an increasingly unpredictable affair. Even simply heading off to work can involve a complex layering procedure designed to account for sudden temperature changes or unforeseen precipitation. At least, though, at home you have all your clothes in one place (the wardrobe for ladies, the devil-may-care pile on the bedroom floor for gentlemen) from which to select the most suitable attire.

If you're on holiday, of course, a whole different set of rules comes into play. You can only wear what you've packed, and you can only pack what you can carry. Consequently, your sartorial palette will consist of little more than quixotic swimwear, Panglossian T-shirts and Wham-esque tennis shorts. Packing for rain bespeaks a defeatism that no self-respecting British subject could bring themselves to display. If the weather should take a turn for the brisk, you will have few options but to remain in your hotel/tent/chalet; if you've stayed inside for too many days – building up a perilous backlog of spending money – and decide to blow a fistful of traveller's cheques on a really nice meal, you won't have anything formal to wear. You couldn't pack a suit or a decent shirt anyway, because the suitcase has yet to be constructed that won't reduce the finest Savile Row tailoring to a sad, crumpled bundle of cloth that looks like Keith Richards has slept in it.

It's a standard joke that American and Japanese tourists in the UK dress really badly. The truth is they have no other choice. Pity them, yes, but for the love of Trinny and Susannah, please don't join them.

Boarding kennels: The unpalatable truth

Last year (or the year before, depending on when you're reading this*) around fifty animals died while being transported around the US by air, with a further twenty or so mysteriously lost (or, for all we know, eaten) by the baggage handlers. International figures are unavailable at the time of writing. Whether those figures are actually secret, or whether it's just because airlines can't be bothered to record how many beloved family pets they kill or eat, is a matter for speculation and the conscience of those fine, fine people at the International Civil Aviation Organisation.

* If you're far enough down the re-gifting chain, it could be the year before that even.

Either way, few people elect to travel with their pet, choosing instead to lodge them in the canine Guantanamo that is the boarding kennel. Perhaps you will have seen an unsteady trestle table erected in your local shopping precinct groaning under the weight of leaflets publicising the horrors of Huntingdon Monkey Prison? Of course, I'm not suggesting for one moment that boarding kennels treat their charges in the same way that the Huntingdon Monkey Prison staff might. Not at all. Boarded pets don't get a fraction of the attention that interned simians do.

With the arguable exception of fish, the animals that live in our homes do so consensually. They could escape pretty much any time they fancied, if they put their minds to it. They live with us because they find the company, catering and central heating rather agreeable. They live in our houses, in short, for exactly the same reasons that we do. If you were to be taken out of your house for a fort-night and placed in a smallish wire cage with only basic food and water to keep you alive and were just walked around an excrement-strewn yard once a day by a friend-less young woman with thick calves, you'd probably be straight on the blower to Amnesty International or Ambulance-Chasers-4U.com or someone. The fact that orange jumpsuits are very much this season's look would probably delay your call for assistance by no more than a day or so. Boarded pets don't even get a jumpsuit. Think it through.

Phrase books and the language barrier

Phrase books are treacherous things. Although of reasonable utility when new, they rapidly deteriorate into a loose-leaf aggregation of potential faux pas after a few days of having been bounced around in a bagful of sweaty cheese sandwiches and pulled out periodically to be stabbed at with a panicky finger. And that's assuming that they haven't been kicked together by an unscrupulous publisher on a budget* who has just popped out in his lunch hour to canvass the staff of his local Starbucks for some exotic sayings. The only phrase book that you can trust implicitly is one produced by Her Majesty's Government and that is, unsurprisingly, targeted mainly at those many unlucky souls who encounter some medical emergency overseas. For more general use, there are simply too many situations for any publication to reliably cover. I've taken something of a shine to you during our little chats, though, which is why I have collected together the three key phrases not to use. Obviously, I'd prefer you not to venture overseas at all, but if you really must, just avoid using any of these popular expressions and you'll be fine.

* Not the fine John Murray company, obviously. Oh no. They're the best. Ask Byron.

Something not to say to a Polish barman: *Proszę oddać mocz do tego naczynia.*

Something not to mention to a group of superstitious Romanian policemen: *Trebuie să vă iau o probă de sânge.*

Something best not to ask a Turkish waiter: *Koyu dışkı gecirdiniz mi?*

Postcards: Why you will never send them

Everywhere you go, shops that sell postcards are easy to spot*: obstructing the public footpath outside every one there will be a (rickety) metal carousel, almost certainly sporting several sharp (tetanus-bearing) protrusions, laden with sun-blanched postcards featuring (unrecognisably idealised) pictures of a local beach at sunset, or (if available) an image of a local landmark taken from a vantage point that is closed to the general public.

Shops selling stamps, though, are rarer, less easy to identify, and do not generally offer such a felicitous retail expe-

---

* If you are lucky enough to be travelling in the Edwardian era, local postcard entrepreneurs will even trot alongside you as you saunter through souks and boulevards, offering you candid portraits of a female relative of theirs. With even Virgin currently not offering a time travel option, this last possibility may, however, remain closed to you for the foreseeable future.

rience. In the postcard shop, you need but pluck a sheaf of likely candidates from the rack and hand it to the shopkeeper, who will relieve you of a surprisingly large bundle of local currency and send you on your way. The foreign post office requires, by contrast, that you display advanced foreign language skills as you express your desire for postage stamps, the destination to which the cards will be sent and the approximate timeframe in which you would prefer your cards to arrive. This last would, of course, be some vague point in the future some weeks after you yourself have returned from your holiday, obliging you to smile wanly as your workmates read back to you the insipid *bons mots* that seemed positively Wildean when you giddily composed them in a Greek taverna, but, in the cold light of fluorescent tubes, seem faintly pathetic when they are revisited a full month after the warm glow of ouzo has left your cheeks.

In summation:

- You probably won't get around to sending any postcards.
- The only postcards you *can* buy will depict a town that bears much the same resemblance to your holiday resort that a Formula One car bears to your dad's Renault Laguna.
- If, by some miracle, you do manage to send one, it will arrive long after you have got home – making you feel extremely silly.

This thesis is easily proven: put a marker in this book, so as not to lose your place (an old postcard will do); go to that drawer where you keep all the takeaway menus, bank statements and other bits of paper that you haven't much use for, but are afraid to throw away; have a good rummage right at the bottom. Is there a postcard? Does it show an idealised sunset over somewhere you went a couple of years ago? Did you forget to send it, and so just brought it home anyway? No, I'm not Derren Brown. I just know about postcards.

THINGS YOU CAN ONLY DO @ HOME #7:
Getting a babysitter in

After marriage, life goes on. Even after parenthood some pitiful semblance of life continues. There are, for example, at least three evenings every year on which you're obliged to squeeze yourself into something uncomfortable and go out for a nice meal*. As long as you remain relatively close to home, all you need to do is book a restaurant and find a local teenager who is willing to find a window in their busy schedule of happy-slapping and self-harm so they can come round and look after your precious progeny. All it's going to cost you is the price of the meal, a couple of taxis,

---

* If you don't know what they are, I'm not going to tell you.

five quid an hour for the babysitter and an eye-watering surprise the next time you get a telephone bill.

Venturing further afield, of course, throws the language barrier into the mix, and whereas teenagers from outside the UK apparently lack the imagination to make low-resolution videos of common assaults or get themselves pregnant at thirteen, there's still something slightly questionable about them. It may be the chain-smoking, it may be the reckless scooter driving. For that matter, it may be a pernicious inability to name more than two *Carry On* films, but whatever otherworldly quality denies them Britishness makes them unsuitable candidates for the immensely important task of caring for your little bundles of noise.

So, if you're going on holiday, you can't have a night out without taking the kids. They'll then get tired in the restaurant and either fall asleep or descend into some kind of blood sugar psychosis, which will put *quite* the crimp in your fantasies of sophisticated Continental dining. If you can't have one nice meal the whole time you're away, it rather throws the whole *raison d'être* of the holiday into a cocked hat, doesn't it? Your other option, of course, is to save a thousand quid or so and go for a blowout meal in that nice little Italian place around the corner. It'll probably have better, more authentically Italian food – with no laminated picture menus – and the waiter will spend more time bringing you food and a little less time leering down your wife's top. Plus, you stand a better chance of getting home to find your kids in one piece and not having been taught to smoke like Alain Delon.

Hair wraps, petty theft, henna tattoos and dysentery: And that's just the highlights

What a great idea. Let's go to a festival this summer. It'll be just like camping*, only worse.

* At your standard European family campsite, there are just the Neolithic conditions and German nudists to torment you. At a festival, you have those, plus trustafarian berks called Jolyon dropping their bloody diablos on your foot every time you venture anywhere near the falafel concession and a couple of his mates playing their bongos until 7 a.m. because they've never had to hold down a proper job in their lives and so the notion of getting to bed at a decent hour is as foreign an idea to them as the idea of being left a rather handsome trust fund is to you. All the time you'll be acutely aware that the bloke at the gate put your wristband on too tightly, and it was OK when it was dry, but now it's a bit damp, you're in danger of losing a hand, but you don't want to say anything in case everyone thinks you've got fat wrists. To make matters worse, some bright spark will invariably have given their dog a corner of blotter acid and the poor piss-sodden creature will crouch trembling in a corner of your tent rolling its eyes and foaming at the mouth while it comes down from The Fear. Don't, whatever you do, get the idea that you'll hear any music either: festivals are invariably sited at the heart of freak weather systems with winds strong enough to whip away the sound of the loudest PA and leave you with nothing but the disconsolate hooting of a damp and disappointed crowd and those incessant fucking bongos.

That lovely couple from Munich: Why you always end up with the Nazis

The thing about fascists is: no one really likes them. Not even their fellow fascists. You only have to look at the fractious relationship between Hitler and Mussolini – who everyone agrees were just about the two top fascists ever – to see what I mean. They had so much in common: Mussolini had an Italian's sense of style, Hitler was always in Hugo Boss. Both of them *adored* invading countries, but they just couldn't get on. Don't get me wrong, they were pals all right – Mussolini was Robin to Hitler's Batman, always getting himself captured and needing rescuing and so forth – but they bickered terribly. Mussolini once privately suggested to Pope Pius XII that he should consider excommunicating Adolf Hitler from the Roman Catholic Church, for example, if you can imagine such a ridiculous thing.

Now the modern fascist is, if anything, *less* likeable than the jackbooted empire-builders of the 1940s. He is unlikely, for example, to be such a snappy dresser. Fascists of today have few, if any, clearly distinguishing sartorial features. You might notice that some senior right-wing fanatics favour those little tasselled loafers or perhaps a blazer, lending them a somewhat nautical appearance*, but otherwise they dress like pretty much anyone else with no time to shop and access to a Racing Green catalogue. Of course, on holiday, even the most liberal soul might inadvertently slip into regatta mode, making Johnny Nazi devilishly hard to spot. So, you can easily find yourself drifting into conversation with a fellow holidaymaker about some innocent topic, like the predictable ineptitude of the holiday rep, or the unfathomable contents of the paella, and, before you know it, he's piped up with some unconscionable opinion on the topic of eugenics or miscegenation or somesuch.

If such a thing should happen at home, perhaps at a first experimental barbecue with a new neighbour, for example, it's a simple enough matter to pretend it didn't happen and simply start getting an earlier train to work in the morning and buying your own strimmer so you never have to deal with the ghastly chap again. In the hothouse confines of a holiday resort, though, you are thrust together by adversity, and it's extremely difficult to politely ignore the fellow – who will generally have an attractively configured but dowdily-dressed wife in tow who mutely shares his Mosleyite delusions and reads *Country Life*. It's a fiendishly tricky business. Your natural politeness will press you to ignore the odious pair until it's time to go home, but then

* Ironic, really. Nazis, like their close relatives, witches, are quite afraid of water. Students of military history will note that the Germans didn't do much in the way of amphibious combat assaults in World War Two and that they wore their Wellingtons even on quite dry days.

you'll find yourself missing out on whatever scant pleasures your holiday *does* have to offer, if you follow that course. Right-wing zealots always seem to frequent the best restaurants, and are fiends for sightseeing. They probably think of it as reconnaissance for *Lebensraum*. And you can't even palm them off on someone else at the same resort, as you might with a party drunk, because, by the time you overcome your entirely laudable British reserve enough to be that rude, the Nazis will have let slip some vile aside about asylum seekers at the wine tasting and everyone else will have clocked their abhorrent politics and have a finely rehearsed array of anti-Nazi excuses prepared. So how best to avoid these nautically dressed terrors and their loathsome opinions? Well, here's a tip: there's aren't all that many Nazis in your front room, you'll find.

A wet weekend in Wallachia

People would have you believe that 70 per cent of the earth is water. Nonsense, of course. The earth is largely dirt, iron and some unknown subterranean melty stuff that nobody really cares about*. Seventy-odd per cent of

* It's probably called McFlurry or something, but you'd have to watch a high-quality educational film like *The Core* for more details on that. This isn't a geology textbook you're holding, you know. Despite all appearances to the contrary.

the earth's *surface*, though, yes – *that*'s covered in water. If the water would only stay where it was supposed to (although, understandably, a certain amount of regrettable inland desertification might ensue), we could have some quite splendid picnics and barbecues. Now, the reason that the nice landy bit of the earth isn't one enormous desert is due, as I'm sure you are aware, to some of the water being vaporised by the sun, coalescing into clouds and then depositing itself very sensibly on Glastonbury. If rainfall could just confine itself to that one irksome tie-dyed police state, everything would be fine, but, unfortunately, precipitation is a rather disorganised affair and appears, broadly speaking, wherever it fancies. In Spain, for example. On the plain, in fact. Despite millennia of scientific effort, we're not much more successful at forecasting the weather than cows are. Or seaweed, come to that. Consequently, rain is effectively impossible to definitively avoid.

In Mexico, India and (my Sunday school teacher assures me) in Bronze Age Israel, people like(d) to make up fancy names for the rains to make them sound more picturesque and to attract tourists, but the fact is that rain's rain, and it's wet and nobody particularly likes being out in it. One of the beauties of the wet weekend at home is that it absolves you of any responsibility to suffer bracing family walks or stultifyingly dull visits to the garden centre and you can get on with the serious business of tearing open a packet of Tunnock's tea cakes and watching *Reach For The Sky* on the telly. If you look away from Kenneth

Moore stumping his way through the Blitz for a moment, you will see from the window that it's still raining *outdoors*, but you're *indoors*, and you may well reflect at this point that life could scarcely be better.

A rainy day when you're on holiday, though, that's quite a different prospect: figures available vary widely, but the average UK household spends at least £650 on a foreign holiday every year (although, bear in mind that the average is pulled down by the growing percentage of the population that has already read this book and very wisely elected to remain at home). Therefore, a day sitting in your villa watching a rain-sodden matador torturing a wet bull on the television amounts to a waste of at least £50. If you're watching a mud-spattered Australian Rules match, then you'll be throwing away closer to £200. Consequently, in the interests of financial prudence, most tourists will drag themselves out in conditions that the locals would consider insufferable and, even on the most inclement days, museums and cathedrals will play host to a grimly determined parade of moist and miserable holidaymakers who smell, collectively, like a damp tramp.

So, unless you have selected central Antarctica as your holiday destination, there is at least some chance of rainfall while you are away. When you are peering over the shoulder of a bulky German at some gloomy oil painting of a miserable-looking Italian bird and someone's cagoule is dripping down the back of your leg, I urge you to think of these things that you have chosen to leave behind: Kenneth More, tea-cakes and Albion.

Bilious hubris: The overseas stag night

The stag night, like democracy, feminism and leaving weak babies out in the cold to die, is a Spartan invention. Their democracy may have withered, but the Spartans' brutality endures in the guise of the Great British Stag Night, which at its historic apogee apparently involved a good deal of dispatching tipsy bachelors to remote train termini and so forth. In the current era, the stag night has become a less savage, but an increasingly expensive affair, bloating from the modest 'two pints of mild and a bag of chips' of the Austerity Years to phenomenally complex overseas trips involving tricky synchronisation of days off, financially perilous one-upmanship with regard to hotel selection and multilingual business transactions with professional ladies of various disciplines. Generally, the focal point of the stag night, the intended groom, will only want a couple of pints of organic lager and a bag of Kettle Chips before going back to the nice little flat he probably already shares with his future bride. Unfortunately, the most sexually dysfunctional of his friends will table a trip to some sex-tourist hotspot like Prague at the planning meeting and everyone else will be too afraid of looking like a lightweight or, worse, a cheapskate, to argue with him and so the motion will pass unopposed. Precious holiday dates will be booked either side of a weekend that, if luck is with them, few will remember. If, by some unlucky chance, they do, then the groom will suddenly have something bigger to worry about than ironing his own shirt on the morning of his wedding.

The best man, having abandoned his own dreams of paintballing or go-karting, will set to the socially awkward task of collecting everyone's deposit and trying to find a hotel that's expensive enough that the attendee who once spilt a mojito on Kate Middleton will be satisfied while still remaining within the budgetary compass of the party member with the large pile of rather stern letters from the Student Loans Company and an unwisely chosen liberal arts degree. The pervert at the heart of the scheme, however, will return to the home he shares with his parents, calculate exactly how many dead-eyed underage East-European hookers he can exploit during one long weekend and dispatch a series of hopeful emails suggesting that perhaps a whole week might be rather more of a lark.

Reading the above, it might all sound rather jolly. Let me assure you, though, that being cautioned by a phlegmatic British bobby for being sick into your own kebab is as nothing compared to the shock of being collared by Cold War-trained Czech police only to find that you've had your wallet lifted by a nimble-fingered Slovak doxy and you have little or no evidence of your identity and no way of explaining the situation to the desk sergeant, who's heard it all before from a thousand other swaying detainees with equally limited language skills. If your idea of a fun weekend is to visit a locale with plentiful clubs, drugs and hookers, I would point out that Moss Side is a cheaper option than Prague or Amsterdam, and, upon your inevitable arrest, you will at least stand half a chance of coming out of the experience without having been brainwashed into assassinating the President of the United States upon hearing a key trigger phrase on the telephone three years hence.

THINGS YOU CAN ONLY DO @ HOME #8:
Having a nice cup of tea

For all its alchemical virtues, the British cuppa is essentially a simple drink: scalding hot water splashed upon a few dried leaves with the admixure of a small amount of (ideally semi-skimmed) milk and there you are. Philistines might advocate a certain amount of sugar in there too, but one rather suspects these are the same yahoos who are in favour of adding curious syrups to coffee in order to make it less coffee-like.

The essential point, though, is that it's a *British* drink. Ask an American to make you a cup of tea and, even after you have negotiated your way through a bewildering choice of 'erb tinctures and described the kind of drink you would like, you will be presented with a greyish liquid capped with a thin slick of scum and, as if that were not bad enough, the tea-bag will be cohabiting with the milk in an entirely unnatural fashion. Now, every British schoolchild knows that the bag shall not lie down with the milk – yea, even in the tea of old ladies it is an abomination – but these precepts are evidently not taught in American High Schools, preoccupied as they are with a much stronger emphasis on areas of academic achievement that British schools tend to neglect. Putting on ad hoc musicals, for example, or marksmanship.

In non English-speaking territories, a decent cup of tea becomes even more elusive. The French, famous for their fine wines and creativity in the kitchen, can no more sort you out a cup of Rosie Lee than they can play cricket, make pop records or win a war against any organisation more heavily armed than Greenpeace. The Germans, meanwhile, will drink coffee, or ersatz coffee even, rather than try tea and, in Scandinavia, the very real danger exists that you may be offered Finnish Christmas Tea, which is universally regarded as the nastiest drink in beverage history and is only drunk by rugby players on a dare who think that chugging a flask of the scrum half's sick isn't enough of a challenge.

The Chinese, for all their vaunted tea-drinking heritage, have no idea what tea is at all and will try to palm you off with some kind of insipid fingerbowl affair to drink. The Japanese, on the other hand, spend so much time fannying about before you actually get your tea that you're generally too distracted by pins and needles in the lower leg to focus on whether the drink passes muster or not. In India, to be fair, you may be able to find a decent cup of tea, but that's a pretty long way to go for something that's not quite as nice as you can get at home. Indian biscuits leave a great deal to be desired as well. Their fig rolls are frankly comical.

You really can't beat a nice drop of Earl Grey, with a dash of milk, in a very thin cup. Packet of Rover assortment on the side and you're set. So why try?

Foreign insects: There's a reason we keep them overseas

I am not one of those foolish people who would have you believe that spiders frequently fall into the mouths of unfortunate sleepers. Spiders, after all, are not fools. They're as reluctant to get eaten as you are, and they avoid gigantic beasts like us whenever they can. Nevertheless, it is an unarguable truth that an assortment of tiny creatures will, at various times, fly or stroll* about your

* You may know, although I frankly hope you don't, that there is an esoteric sexual aberration called Formicophilia which calls for a number of ants (or, if wet, beetles) crawling on the progenitive member (or thereabouts) of the enthusiast. It has, let me assure you, nothing to do with 1970s kitchen worktops.

domicile, especially if you have a garden. As long as you live in the UK, though, the operative word is tiny: most of these little blighters can be easily dispatched with a well-placed slipper or (if at altitude) the local paper should they outstay their welcome.

The same benign conditions do not prevail overseas. The Atlas Moth, for example, is up to a foot across. You'd have trouble taking one of those bastards down with a rolled-up *Bromley Advertiser*, assuming you could even get hold of a copy in its Indonesian, Sri Lankan or Malaysian habitat. The Acteon Beetle, which hangs around South America, can reach four inches in length and an inch and a half in thickness. And it isn't even the largest South American beetle. There are even unconfirmed reports of a nine-inch monster beetle in remoter parts ** and, frankly, that's the best place for it.

Except for a very small team imprisoned in Regent's Park zoo for a crime they didn't commit, there are no gigantic insects living in the British Isles today. That's just as it should be. The mess a foot-wide moth would leave should you chance to splatter it on your chimney breast barely bears thinking about. It's the work of an unbalanced mind, then, to remove oneself from these

** No matter what your predilections, you would no more want *that* beast striding along your Johnson (or, if you are a lady, in amongst your furbelow) than you would want the late Bernard Manning sharing your bath. Even if he kept his pants on.

comparatively insect-free shores and travel (often at great expense) to locales where the discovery of a good-sized scorpion in one's sleeping bag is as routine a matter as accidentally stepping in a dog egg might be on Streatham High Street. You will also not need to be reminded, I am sure, that female mosquitoes of the genus Anopheles, being the chief vector of malaria, have been responsible for more human deaths than all the lions, tigers and high-kicking kung fu maniac robot dinosaurs that have ever lived put together.

Some people are less squeamish about our arthropod cousins than others, but it's hard to be sanguine about a bug that's bigger than your hand. If you visit the homes of these freakish creatures, know that you do it without my blessing.

14 days in purdah: Why foreigners think all British women are easy

Foreign people must just be more interested in sex than us. That's all there is to it. In Great Britain, a woman of almost any age can go out dressed as a Bratz doll and spend the whole night drinking Bacardi Breezers without attracting a second glance. Unless she's pulled off the Bratz doll look *especially* well, then she might elicit a muted cheer from the two remaining Englishmen working on a building site. Abroad, though, different conditions apply. In Saudi Arabia, for example, the men are such seething volcanoes of passion that all the women have to dress as Batman all the time to dampen their ardour and no one's allowed so much as a Pimms on a warm day. And they have a *lot* of warm days. In Italy, too, although the younger ladies dress a little more flamboyantly than their Arabian cousins, by ancient Roman law every woman must morph instantly upon reaching her thirtieth birthday into a pasta-fuelled version of the Grandma from a Giles cartoon. This tends to rather skew the overall average of attractiveness downwards. As a consequence, Italian men are commonly stirred into priapic frenzies by the sight of a visiting shapely British bottom (half-covered with a Primark pelmet in the traditional Novocastrian fashion) and will be unable to resist puttering along the pavement on their funny little disability scooters in order to catch up with and playfully pinch the callipygian wonder.

British women are (quite properly) accorded much the same freedoms as their male counterparts. *More* freedoms in some ways, as an Englishman dressed as a Bratz doll will often, as I have found to my cost, draw the occasional acerbic comment in the tennis club bar. In accordance with Moran's Law, as previously discussed, most popular holiday destinations are situated at a distance from Highgate Village, which places them in the years before the dawn of female emancipation and, as a consequence, women visiting these benighted locations are advised by our local diplomatic missions to wear a great more to the local cantinas or trattorias then they might on an average night out in one of our free-thinking All Bar Ones.

The thing is, the only reason that we visit these countries of which I speak is that they're a bit warm – so, of course, any right-thinking woman is going to feel inspired to wear, if anything, a little *less* than she normally might. To her stolid British male companion, of course, this will make hardly any difference at all, as his native British decency, tolerance and sexlessness will inure him to the temptations of all that extra flesh. To Johnny Foreigner, by contrast, the same casual mode of attire is regrettably an incitement to riot. An ensemble as modest as, say, a stylish and practical PVC nurse's uniform from Britain's favourite designer, Ms Ann Summers, can quite easily precipitate a diplomatic incident.

Mind you, because everyone except us is defaulting on the Kyoto agreement, Britain's warming up anyway. So why not spend a fortnight in your own garden and dress as sluttily as you like? The only people that will know or care will be your gamekeeper and those fine people who man the satellite cameras at Google Maps.

THINGS YOU CAN ONLY DO @ HOME #9:
Read the papers

Even today, with circulations plummeting and levels of literacy returning to pre-Renaissance levels, settling down to read the Sunday papers is one of the most splendid treats imaginable. Topped off with a bacon sandwich and a second cup of coffee, there really is no better way to start the Sabbath. The exact news source you select isn't all that important* (although close observers of the once-popular and still marvellous television series *Yes, Prime Minister* might suggest it is) and even flopping back into bed with a *National Enquirer* and a Lemsip will do. It's the sheer luxury of having no plans for the next few hours, access to sachet-free tea and coffee making facilities, and something to read that has loads of surplus sections that you can just throw away that's important. Who cares about Business on a Sunday? Sport, yes, but Jobs? Who thinks about work on a Sunday? (Well, apart from vicars, obviously.) Don't even start me on the Travel section! What you want is a little bit of news, some reviews of

---

* I, of course, take *The Times*, for reasons which keen-eyed readers will surely deduce, and I'm quite fond of *Heat*, but I'd rather read the fire instructions on the hotel door again than try to tease some sense out of the *Florida Union Jack*.

shows you can't be bothered to attend and an idea of what's on the telly later. A healthy dollop of scandal never hurt a Sunday rag either, but even the broadsheets have a bit of that tucked away somewhere if you know where to look. If you don't know where to look, just slip last week's *Heat* inside your *Sunday Telegraph* and you'll be fine.

The thing is, as a thousand biltong-skinned expats will tell you, you really can't get a nice proper Sunday paper anywhere else in the world. Indeed, getting any UK newspaper that doesn't feel suspiciously thin is tricky enough. That's why, on the flight back, there's a mad scramble for the slightly dog-eared copies of the *Daily Mail* that have been left down the back of the seats. You may think you don't care about current affairs but, if you're out of the loop for a couple of weeks, you start to feel a strange sensory deprivation. No one can last more than a few days without an update on what's happening in *Big Brother*, or who Calum Best is dating, that kind of thing. Things happen in the grown-up news that are slightly interesting too, now and again. Seemingly on a whim, the government changes things, laws and stuff, which might have some relevance to your life if you only understood them. Every British newspaper explains the complicated law stuff in the way most likely to mean something to their particular class of reader, but you can't expect to catch up with two weeks' homework in just one read, and, sure enough, the government will be changing more laws tomorrow, so you're more or less obliged to hang around fairly close to home if you don't want to spend the rest of the summer looking like a simpleton who hasn't bothered to do any revision.

 So:

No holiday = Relaxing on the bed with a loved one, an enormous paper with extra sections you can use to line the budgie cage, and coffee and orange juice etc.
Holiday = Getting back to work and not knowing what the hell everyone's talking about and having to pretend to understand the topical gags on Jonathan Ross for the next couple of weeks.

Not the trickiest choice, is it?

You've got to pick a pocket or two. Or several more than two, if you're a Spaniard

You might think, from having read so far, that I haven't got a good word to say for our overseas cousins. That would be an error. There are some things done abroad to a standard that we plucky Brits could never match. To select just one example: pickpocketing.

Now, in the UK, pickpocketing is one of those skills, like thatching or blacksmithery, that's rather gone out of style with the native population. In Charles Dickens's day, teams of young entrepreneurs scoured the cities dressed as Russell Brand, lifting silk handkerchiefs from the pockets of the gentry on a more-or-less 24/7 basis. Now, for the most part, the market for other peoples' snot has rather fallen off and the market focus for light-fingered teenagers lies much more in the area of pre-owned electrical goods.

In other countries, by contrast, the appetite for dipping an optimistic hand into a stranger's pocket remains undimmed. There are some thoroughfares in popular holiday destinations down which you can stroll in the confident expectation of having the very fluff from your pockets removed by true masters of the dipper's art. Las Ramblas, in Barcelona, is but one case in point: on a fine summer's evening one might walk the entire length of the thoroughfare without finding someone who is not either tourist, thief or bloody annoying pretend-statue man. Indeed, in the low season, Spanish pickpockets are reduced to rifling through each other's pockets just to keep their hand in, so to speak. And there are other boulevards further abroad where matters are considerably worse.

Your only defence against these sticky-fingered knaves appears to be to place all objects of value into a bum-bag and wear it (against all good fashion sense) for the entire duration of your stay in whichever benighted nest of thieves to which you have inadvertently confined yourself. Well, if you choose to disport yourself looking like a particularly paunchy kangaroo, I very much fear that you may be beyond even my help.

A souvenir you didn't expect: The humble bedbug

These islands in which we live have many admirable qualities, but first among them is, perhaps, that they are islands. A broad expanse of water defends us against all but the most determined invaders from Europe, and the mighty Atlantic is an impregnable bulwark against opportunistic coyote or raccoon attacks from the left-hand side of the map. Regrettably, these natural advantages are being increasingly subverted by the availability of cheap air travel, so a growing number of nasty and unattractive creatures are establishing a bridgehead for invasion. Grizzly bears and komodo dragons are not, as yet, frequent flyers but smaller, more insidious foes are already among us: the incidence of bedbug infestations around our major airports has risen by about 80 per cent in the last twelve months alone.

Now, there are a great many myths about bedbugs (or is that dragons?). There is certainly a traditional belief that bedbugs are sort of pikey and that only rather dirty people have them*. Unfortunately, our current climate of woolly liberal modern relativism brings many people to reject that view. However, I would like to propose, if I may, some middle ground between these two poles of

---

* I think you have to be *insanely* dirty to get dragons.

opinion: anyone, no matter what their standard of personal hygiene or political convictions may be, can *get* bedbugs, but they can only *catch* them off someone who is really, really pikey. The concentration of these vile beasts around London and Manchester's airports should be evidence enough to support my hypothesis: bedbugs are being imported from all those nasty hot countries where outposts of The Body Shop are in short supply. Time was, of course, when families would fly in splendidly appointed jets with a bath each and a small soapy pillow of Cussons' Imperial Leather with which to repel any microscopic stowaways. Now, of course, travellers are packed into aircraft like so many plates in a dishwasher and not even the pilot gets a bath. You can't even wash your hands, nine times out of ten, because there's invariably some misguided couple trying to make the two-backed beast in the cramped and malodorous toilet.

Anyway, here are some facts about bedbugs:

They reproduce in a truly horrible way The male makes a hole in the female and squirts his seed into it without worrying too much if she enjoys that kind of thing or even if she's altogether awake. They'll even punch a hole in the bodies of other male bedbugs and ejaculate into that, just on spec. Poor form, I say.

The way they eat is pretty vile too They have two little tubes, one to dispense a sort of anticoagulant venom/ BBQ relish and the other to suck blood out of the victim's body. You may disagree, and that is, of course, your right, but I believe that living on another living being's blood is a pretty rum show.

Some fairly disquieting pathogens have been detected living inside bedbugs' bodies, including the plague virus and Hepatits B Bedbugs have not been definitively linked to the transmission of any disease and are not currently regarded by our do-gooding 'innocent until proven guilty' medical profession as a plague carriers. Not *currently*, that is. Please bear in mind that there was a point in history when cigarettes weren't *conclusively* linked to lung cancer and even (for all I know) a time when being smacked over the head with a sword wasn't *definitively* linked to decapitation.

Just because someone hasn't been actually caught doing something, though, isn't any reason to stop suspecting them. Personally, I remain suspicious of any creature that treats me as a walking black pudding buffet, and any one of those facts should be enough to convince you that you don't want one of these things living in your mattress.

In the days of horse-drawn transport and coaching inns, when fine quality shower gel was harder to come by in Britain and bedbugs were consequently rife, travellers would carry a piglet with them to place in each bed they slept in before retiring so that the local bedbugs could sate themselves on pigs' blood and therefore not bite the piglet owner. You could, I suppose, try a similar trick today: just list the hotels and guesthouses that you could stay in, don't stay in them, and then let some holidaymaking dimwit who hasn't read this book get his hard-earned blood sucked out instead. Meanwhile, you can remain in your own bed, with no more creatures in it than you choose to have, and with your own bathroom nearby in case you should chance, for some unknown reason, to get dirty in some way.

5 reasons why everybody hates a tourist

1 Money

Wherever you're going, it's a safe bet that you've got more disposable income than most of the people who live there. The farther you go, the greater the disparity will grow. Now, money isn't everything, but it can more or less *buy* everything, and so it ends up figuring rather significantly in the minds of people who haven't got so much of it. I'm not suggesting that your squandering conspicuous sums of money on international travel will engender the sort of resentment that, say, the self-indulgence of the French royal court did in 1789, or the lavish excesses of the Russian aristocracy in 1917, of course. No, not a bit of it. The fops and dandies in question interacted very little with the peasantry, yet still annoyed them enough to precipitate a bloody revolution. Tourists are there in the people's face every day for the whole bloody summer. Which leads us to . . .

2 Luggage

A lot of foreign travel involves cities. Even if you think you're going to a bit of exotic countryside, you're bound to end up flying into an airport on the fringes of some major conurbation and then getting a train or taxi through the city centre to your destination. Let's hope it is a taxi, because that's just an annoying car like so many others and unlikely to give rise to too much smouldering resentment. If you're on a train or an underground system of some sort, you'll be dragging assorted pieces of bulky luggage around with you, scuffing the shins of pedestrians with your suitcase, obliviously crushing the newspapers of tube travellers with your rucksack or tripping absolutely everybody up with one of those spectacularly annoying trolley-bag affairs. You may think that you're having enough trouble struggling from airport to hotel or train terminus, but the people you're inadvertently barging into are on their way to or from work, and were probably in a fairly bad mood *before* you clattered into them with your skis. Which rather calls to mind . . .

3 Congestion

The joy, such as it is, of visiting a foreign city is stopping to look up at the interesting architectural features, unexpected poor weather or strange and unusual birds that are about to defecate on your head. The drawback to these simple pleasures, of course, is that, every time you stop to rubberneck at an exotic-looking and mildly pornographic advertising hoarding you will cause a concertina of collisions in the 'long tail' of fast-moving locals behind you who have seen all this stuff before and are just trying to get to where they're going before the monsoon rains kick in. Which naturally takes us to . . .

4 Time

Being on holiday, you've got lots of it. The people you're asking for directions, however, have little or none. The people behind you in the queue for overpriced cups of coffee have even less. Words do not exist to describe the depth of their hatred for you. Please remember that, in many other countries, knives and guns are more commonly carried than they are in, say, Royal Tunbridge Wells. Which takes us rather neatly to . . .

5 Money (again)

The presence of a large group of people with substantial amounts of disposable income, generous amounts of leisure time to fill and no way of storing or cooking fresh food tends to skew the local economy somewhat in the direction of overpriced coffee or sandwich bars and expensive clothing shops. Exactly the opposite of what you need if you actually live in one of these places, where all you want is a sensibly priced pastie to reheat in the office microwave for your lunch, a reasonably-priced dry cleaners and somewhere to buy an emergency present for your wife's birthday, and you're not made of bloody money and you've only got an hour to eat, get your suit cleaned and buy the Smallest Diamond On Earth™.

A surprisingly convenient truth

If you're the impressionable sort who believes holiday adverts, you might be tempted to leave the UK in search of fine weather. Depending on exactly which bit of it you live in, that might be a mistake. There *is* a fair bit of rain driven into the country by the south-western trade winds following the warm Gulf Stream currents, of course. Areas along the western coasts (Ireland, Wales, Cornwall – the bits of Britain people tend go on holiday in) can receive between 1016 and 2540 mm of rain annually. That's pretty wet. Any holiday there would be likely to be blighted by at least one day trapped in a guest-house (or, worse, tent) listening to Elaine Paige singing selections from the musicals. However, what the people who sell those climate-changing flights out of the country don't want you to know is that the eastern and southern parts of the UK (where most of the people actually *live*) are significantly drier, with the South East having a lower average rainfall than Jerusalem or Beirut, only receiving between

450 and 600 mm of rain per year. Mooching around at home might be the cleverest thing you ever do.

Internet cafés: The last refuge of the workaholic

There is a new breed of buffoon abroad in the world of work today. The man (or, quite possibly, woman) who believes himself (or herself) so entirely dispensable at his (or her) place of work that he feels (I'll stop that now, just let's agree that we're fully supportive of everyone's equal opportunity to make poor decisions about their work/life balance) obliged to surround himself with mobile phones, Blackberry devices, pagers and other assorted appurtenances designed to maintain constant contact with the mighty employer in case some pressing matter should arise during *Steve Wright's Sunday Love Songs* that requires the urgent personal attention of that particular wage slave.

Of course, many of these electronic gadgets, like their close relatives the electronic tags administered for the Home Office by those fine people at Group 4 Security, cease to function overseas, leading to debilitating withdrawal symptoms for the woebegone employee. There is solace, though, in the Internet café.

Visit any of these overpriced, poorly appointed establishments in the high holiday season and you will see dozens of still-pallid faces bathed in the tell-tale off-white glow that bespeaks a computer displaying Microsoft Outlook Web Access.

We've all done it. We're all probably going to do it again. You might even be doing it right now. There's only one question really. Haven't you got a computer at home?

TRAVEL TIPS #5:
AUSTRALIA – Snakebite isn't just a drink

You have but to order a drink in any London bar to know the truth. Australia is empty. The entire population of that island continent is over here telling us all how great Australia is and serving us drinks. Or (increasingly) drilling holes in our teeth. Or (I have noticed of late) attending to the health of our pets. So why, do you think, would an entire generation of Australians leave their homes and travel over halfway around the world to live on an island that (they constantly remind us) is small, damp, dirty and cold?

Because of the snakes.

If you count sea snakes in the surrounding waters (and you might as well), there are over 170 species of snake native to Australia. Not all of them are poisonous. Most are, though: at least one hundred of those species can give you a bite that you will definitely not enjoy and twelve are quite capable of killing you, should the necessity arise. Taipans are among the nastiest. One variant, reassuringly called the Fierce Snake, is about as poisonous as anything needs to be: a single bite from one contains enough venom to kill as many as one hundred adult humans. And it's even more dangerous to mice, my boffins tell me. Fortunately, they aren't all that common*. By contrast, the King Brown Snake can be found almost anywhere in Australia with enough space to hide a three-metre-long reptile and, although his poison has only about a quarter of the toxicity of its rarer cousin, it's still quite potent enough to ensure that you shan't be needing the return portion of your ticket should a King Brown take a sudden dislike to you.

Clearly, the only person that should be planning a trip to that most distant of destinations is St Patrick. The rest of us should just rejoice in the plentiful supply of bar staff, vets and dentists concomitant with an almost entirely snake-free environment.

---

* This is snakes, not boffins. There's plenty of boffins. Not a week goes by without another bunch of chaps in white coats writing in to the *Daily Star* and telling us they've discovered something astounding about Ovaltine or something.

On a barge? How to endure the smell

Given the unalloyed horrors incipient in a foreign holiday, you might, in a weak moment, consider an old-school putter around the Norfolk Broads. Norfolk, best known for its celebrated turkey prisons and complete lack of discernible landscape, also has a tremendous swathe of bog and marsh that we have all agreed to generously describe as 'wetlands'. These wetlands are the habitat of a colossal population of geese, each and every one of which will make it a priority to crap on your rented barge at least once a day, rendering the deck treacherously slippery even for a sober person, let alone someone who has spent the entire night drinking beer that smells like a bad egg just to get in out of the cold.

You, of course, will not crap on your barge even once a day if you can help it. The vile miasma of chemical toilet stink will waft around the lower cabin even after the most ladylike visit, forcing you to sit up on deck in the drizzle and goose guano for the greater part of the day. There'll be nothing much to see, though, except for the occasional hexadactyl child of incest standing on the bank and pointing at you with one of his supernumerary digits. Strangers are still very much a source of wonder in the wilder parts of Norfolk.

As a consequence (as on so many holidays), you will drink, and drink to excess, to numb the boredom.

Guidebooks will extol the virtues of the plentiful Adnams pubs in the region, but somehow, when the persistent drizzle soaks through your last dry T-shirt and you drag your sodden family ashore for a pub lunch, the nearest inn will inexplicably be a Tolly Cobbold franchise. Tolly Cobbold is a near-undrinkable Suffolk ale made of yeast, hops, barley and powdered egg. Drinkers who can somehow manage to ignore the distasteful smell long enough to swallow a few mouthfuls of the stuff will soon come to wish they didn't when it plays its deleterious tricks on the digestion that no chemical toilet as yet devised by the mind of man can hope to contain.

In desperation, by the end of week one, most Broads holidaymakers have moved on to spirits to keep out the all-pervading chill. It's around the beginning of week two, therefore, that they have their first significant collision with another slow, unresponsive, inadequately insured vessel piloted by another tipsy novice. Then the fun begins.

Benedict Arnold knew my father: 11 sure-fire ways to offend an American

Whether travelling to Florida in pursuit of the great god, Mickey Mouse, or squeezing between two corn-fed Minnesotans in the Sistine Chapel, you're going to encounter a lot of Americans on holiday. If you've already booked, it's probably too late to back out, so you might as well have *some* fun: you might as well annoy an American. The first and most reliable way to annoy an American is to patronise him culturally. They're used to it but they still can't stand it. Wrinkle your lip and mutter the word 'oxymoron' if they dare use the term 'Great American Novel', for example. If that doesn't tip them over the edge, here's a list of the eleven topics most likely to endanger the Special Relationship:

1 Food and Nutrition
Our colonial cousins are fairly sensitive with regard to food. Whereas there is a thin fringe of tofu-eating nut-burger self-flagellators around the edges of North America, years of childishly self-indulgent gorging have returned most residents of the continental interior to an infantile state of helpless cuddliness. They have vast refrigerators the size of a bijou London studio flat and every corner of these gigantic edifices is packed with sugary, salty comfort-eating adult baby food that's composed mostly of pow-dered heart attack. They know it, and they don't like it. They still can't do anything about it, though. They just can't say no to a chimichanga. The little fat fatties.

2 English Literature
If you should encounter the rare *brainy* American, they'll be too clever to fall into the standard T. S. Eliot trap, so it's always worthwhile trying to tease them about

Hemingway instead. His clipped, chippy, calliboguscrazed style has inspired virtually every American writer since into shaping a novel like it was a telegram from the boys' changing room. The underlying theme of every single book he wrote was 'Ooh! look at me! I'm a man! I've probably got a penis!' There's such a thing as protesting too much, you know, Ernie. Let it go. After all, look at me: I've got to more or less the middle of this book and I haven't told you about how manly I am once, have I? Although I am *quite* manly. *And* I'm having an alcoholic drink while I'm writing this. It's only a shandy, admittedly, but it's a very warm afternoon.

3 Media Studies

Of course, in the world of cinema, there have been some great Americans over the years. Why, just take a brief look at some legends who made Hollywood what it is today: Charlie Chaplin, Stan Laurel, Bob Hope, Boris Karloff, Cary Grant and Elizabeth Taylor, to name but a few. All English born, of course, but we're decent enough to let America borrow a bit of our talent until they get their little movie business on its feet. Michael Caine, Christian Bale, Tim Roth, Gary Oldman, Orlando Bloom, to name but a few more. Keira Knightley, even.

4 Politics

Flawed as it is, Britain's parliament is the model to which all other political systems aspire. Although its meritocratic ideal of 'cleverest person in the country gets to decide everything' is more commonly downgraded to 'most persuasive double-glazing salesman wins', it's still leagues ahead of America's primitive 'OK, buddy, how much power can you afford?' model. Even the dimmest, tubbiest American feels an occasional twinge of shame at the thumb-fingered attempts of successive administrations to imitate Britain's avuncular imperial style of foreign policy. We always managed to patronise the natives of countries we invaded in a way that made them want to be us. American imperialists just get on everybody's nerves and make them want to blow stuff up.

5 Geography

Americans are notoriously vague on geography. The average European, principally, it must be said, by dint of having watched far too many terrible films, can produce a vague outline of the USA, identify most of the principal cities and make a reasonable stab at doing the accent. Because very few Americans travel outside the borders of the continental United States, except for purposes of waging war, they simply don't know where most places are. Which, you might suggest, rather invalidates their position as the World's Police. After all, providing directions should be a copper's basic skill. Ask them to point Iraq out on a map. They love that.

6 History

As flaky as Americans are on geography, they're twice as bad at history. Perhaps it's because they haven't really got any. Years of exposure to dubiously researched anti-British films starring Mel Gibson or rankly inaccurate pro-American films starring Enigma machines has rather skewed the perception of recent events in the American's mind in favour of flag-waving nonsense in which all the villains sound a bit like Alan Rickman. Which last part, in fairness, is substantially true.

7 Military History

For a nation that's been at war more or less constantly since its inception (apart from the obvious ones, like Independence, Civil, WWI, WWII, Korea, Vietnam, Iraq, etc., they've also had minor contretemps with the Spanish, Mexicans, Canadians, the Grenadians, or whatever they're called, and, most perplexingly, drugs). Every time they've either turned up late or left early. They like to think they're tough, but they're far better at shooting their own side than anyone else. Candidly, for such a heavily-armed nation, they're a gang of light-weights.

8 Art

My *word*, the Yanks are rubbish at painting. Yes, Whistler wasn't bad, but he had to come to the UK to work. They like to claim John Singer Sargent too, but he was essentially a European painter with an American dad. Not the same thing as being American at all. On that basis, we could claim George Washington. Rauschenberg, Jasper Johns, Pollock – daubers to a man. Americans are, against all likelihood, even worse at painting than they are at making tea. And they're godawful at that.

9 Sport
Or, if they insist, 'Sports'. Any country that hosts a 'World Series' that no one else is allowed to enter has to be considered rather questionable in the field of athletic endeavour. Rather than play rugby, they have their own curious variant wherein everyone stuffs pillows down their pyjamas and wears a cycling helmet in case they get hurt. And a nation that size ought to produce at least eleven world-class 'soccer' players a year. Instead they produce an endless cavalcade of donkeys who are even worse at football, if you can imagine such a thing, than I am.

10 The Irish question
Americans revere and irrationally mythologise Ireland like no other rain-soaked bit of dirt on earth. Yet they don't understand the long and complex shared history that Britain and Eire share and they don't respect the Black Drink enough to keep green dye out of it. No matter how they pretend, not one of them is half as Irish as Hitler. Or as well-dressed, come to that.

11 Music
No matter what that fat lad in a checked shirt you shared a room with at university said, American music is rubbish. As a result of the more plentiful bars with live music

over there, there are more opportunities for US-based musicians to perform in front of an audience, so they get a lot more practice than ours, but knowing the most chords is not what it's all about. Having an original idea in your head is the really key part: no one wants to buy a record they've already got. Elvis Presley, the quintessential American rock 'n' roll star, was really just an Otis Blackwell tribute act that got lucky. And he was the best of them: virtually every hit US rock or pop act of the last fifty-odd years has taken either an American R&B combo that didn't sell any records because they were a bit too tanned-looking or (more commonly) a British band as their inspiration. Generally, you'll find that the wonderful, but not entirely original Led Zeppelin is the band in question, but you may find the odd Beatles tribute band too. The more adventurous US musicians avoid aping a UK group by looking slightly further afield for their inspiration. They generally look as far as Dublin before getting bored and learning some U2 songs. A clever interlocutor might possibly point out The Velvet Underground as a counter to your argument, at which point you can point out the nationality of the multi-instrumentalist who gave them their unique sound and get back to eating your chimichanga.

One last word

Americans do go on rather about firearms, and tend to carry one about their person at all times. Before you engage one of them in friendly banter about how rubbish their country is, be sure to check that his fingers are too chubby to fit through the little trigger thingy.

Honeymoon mosquito safari

All the best sociologists agree that marriage is, despite the ever-growing list of alternatives, the best way to cement a society. Sooner or later even the most self-consciously 'alternative' couples cave in to the combination of romance, peer pressure and sheer naked desire for a good old-fashioned knees-up. Even if it takes place in a field near Stonehenge, and the celebrant is dressed as a clown, it still counts.

And once the wedding is over, what could be more natural than to go on a lovely holiday with your loved one?

Even if, as is so often the case these days, you have been shacked up with your spouse for some time prior to the happy occasion, you will feel compelled to . . . well . . . I hardly know how to put this: to hoick up the wedding dress and go at it like knives for a little while. And so you should. You aren't going to get that kind of action on holiday, though, and here's why.

There is an occult alchemy that takes place in a warm marital bed. The combination of high temperatures, the mysteriously musky scent of humanity at play and a darkened room is seemingly irresistible to the family

Culicidae. The new groom will, if he has been unwise enough to book a honeymoon anywhere south of the 45th parallel, spend every night of the romantic break capering naked around a hotel bedroom waving an ichor-splattered Rough Guide trying to reduce the mosquito population of the chamber to double figures in a quixotic attempt to restore (however fleetingly) an erotic ambience to the Honeymoon Suite. Unfortunately, the undignified spectacle of a grown man chasing mosquitoes around the room with his gentleman's gentleman penduluming like some peculiarly hair-fringed fairground ride will, regrettably, tend to have a somewhat deleterious effect on female desire after the first hour or so. Don't worry, though. The laughter should have more or less abated by the time you clear customs.

10 movie myths about holidays, and the awful truth behind them

Filmmakers seem to be, as often as not, in league with the travel industry in a way that frankly makes one feel a trifle suspicious. For every hard-hitting documentary like *Frantic* or *Don't Look Now* there are a dozen rose-tinted travelogues representing holidays as times when nice things happen. It isn't entirely clear why these two ostensibly rival leisure industries are apparently collaborating to perpetrate this outrageous canard, but I am here to set the record straight. For example:

1: The Lie: It never rains in southern California
The Movies: *Bullitt*, *The Graduate*, *The Wedding Planner*
The Truth: Although San Francisco is sited at a comparatively temperate 38 degrees north, being surrounded on three sides by water makes it prone to bitter winds and frequent rain showers, interrupted only by impenetrable fog. Mark Twain probably *didn't* say 'The coldest winter I ever spent was a summer in San Francisco.' But someone did, and with good reason. It's like Glasgow, just with slightly better car chases. Avoid.

2: The Lie: Holiday romances are a good thing
The Movies: *Dirty Dancing*, *Roman Holiday*, *The Holiday*
The Truth: As discussed elsewhere: best case, a treatable rash. Worst case: stalker, tug-of-love custody battle, honour killing.

3: The Lie: A summer holiday with a large group of friends won't involve any arguments or robberies, instead you'll all have a crazy time hosting keggers in your surprisingly capacious and apparently self-cleaning beach house and losing your virginity to leggy bisexual lingerie models who think you're cute.
The Movies: *American Pie*, *American Pie 2*, *Lemon Popsicle*

The Truth: You are a group of spotty teenage boys and you have absolutely no chance of getting served in an off licence, let alone having a life-affirming sexual awakening involving leggy models in Agent Provocateur knickers.

4: The Lie: Sex on the beach is a joyous life-enhancing experience
The Movie: *From Here To Eternity*
The Truth: Sand really does get everywhere.

5: The Lie: Australia is full of fun-loving and terribly witty homosexual gentlemen
The Movies: *Muriel's Wedding*, *Priscilla Queen of the Desert*, *Strictly Ballroom*
The Truth: If the snakes don't get you, the pathologically homophobic Aussie Rules football players will.

6: The Lie: Paris is a romantic and beautiful city, where magical things happen
The Movies: *French Kiss*, *Moulin Rouge*, *Charade* and about a billion others
The Truth: You'll be too busy looking down at your feet to avoid getting dog crap on your slingbacks to consider looking up at the stars for a moment.

7: The Lie: Ireland is a whimsical isle of leprechauns and holy drinkers
The Movies: *The Quiet Man*, *The Match Maker*

The Truth: It's raining pretty much all the time on the Emerald Isle. That's why it's so bloody Emerald. If you think it's depressing being there for a week, try spending your whole life there. You won't feel too whimsical after the first couple of waterlogged summers, I can assure you.

8: The Lie: Picking up a hitchhiker on a driving holiday will end in a touching romance
The Movie: *Summer Holiday*
The Truth: Someone who's looking for a free ride is looking for a *free ride*. They will steal your wallet the minute you stop to do a dance routine next to your bus.

9: The Lie: When driving across America you will meet a non-stop parade of entertaining eccentrics who will want to be your friend
The Movies: *Cannonball Run, It's a Mad Mad Mad Mad World, The Great Race*
The Truth: On the rare occasions that you see anyone at all in America's near-deserted heartland, they will almost certainly be a heavily-armed White Supremacist weirdo who wants to lock you in a cupboard with a view to eventually wearing your skin as a suit. And that's if you're lucky.

10: The Lie: A holiday in the south of France will be so marvellous that it will lead you to actually *move* to Pro-bloody-vence to run a quaint vineyard with stereotypical locals wearing strings of garlic around their neck who will lead you to a Damascene conversion from the ways of Mammon and a realisation that the only way to find true love and fulfilment is by living on a smallholding and eating nothing but ripe brie like some kind of cheese-crazed Hugh Fearnley-Whittingstall

The Movie: *A Good Year*

The Truth: Your money will be hoovered up by local red tape and dodgy builders, all the local officials will be on their lunch break between 10 a.m.–4 p.m. and, before you know how much trouble you've got yourself into, you'll be broke and back in the UK living in your mother's garage.

Row 29

Urban legends. Where would we be without them? Well, in pretty much the same place, actually, just with a bit less email. One story that did the rounds of slackers' inboxes a little while back bears repeating. First, because it gives you an insight into air operators' attitude to their customers. Second, because, unlike many of the warnings about flashing your headlights in Florida or once-in-a lifetime financial opportunities in Nigeria, it's true. Or, at least, truer than the one about being bought a drink in a hotel bar and then waking up in the bath one kidney lighter.

A passenger on a Continental Airlines flight out of Houston, Texas, was assigned the end seat of row 29 on a Boeing 737-800. It's a good seat in many ways: it's at the back for a start – and, as every comic writer since Aristophanes has pointed out, aircraft don't often *reverse* into mountains – plus it's handy for the toilets.

It was this very handiness, though, that was at the root of the problem for the hero of our tale. Seat 29E was, if anything, a little *too* handy for the toilets. I quote here from his original letter of complaint, which was written during the flight and what it lacks in literary finesse it fully makes up for with its immersive reportage:

Dear Continental Airlines,

I am disgusted as I write this note to you about the miserable experience I am having sitting in seat 29E on one of your aircraft. As you may know, this seat is situated directly across from the lavatory, so close that I can reach out my left arm and touch the door.

All my senses are being tortured simultaneously. It's difficult to say what the worst part about sitting in 29E really is! Is it the stench of the sanitation fluid that's blown all over my body every 60 seconds when the door opens? Is it the whoooosh of the constant flushing? Or is it the passengers' asses that seem to fit into my personal space like a pornographic jig-saw puzzle?

Our plucky hero goes on to point out that he paid in excess of $400 for the experience. Given that the whole sorry business took place in late 2004, I would imagine the same olfactory thrill-ride would cost rather more today. At the time of writing the 737-800 is still in service on that route. It's not all bad news, though. In a demonstration of the MacGyver spirit that ennobles us all, he improvised a partial defence:

> I constructed a stink-shield by shoving one end of a blanket into the overhead compartment – while effective in blocking at least some of the smell, and offering a small bit of privacy, the ass-on-my-body factor has increased, as without my evil glare, passengers feel free to lean up against what they think is some kind of blanketed wall. The next ass that touches my shoulder will be the last!

Continental's response when asked about the veracity of this complaint was a light-hearted parade of lame puns that, rather than conjuring a heartfelt expression of regret, might more properly find their home in a slim volume of gentle humour. Which is rather convenient, because that's where they are now:

> The letter is not totally accurate and uses sarcastic humor to make the seat sound a lot worse than it is. But we don't want to pooh-pooh this customer's concerns – seat 29E is less than ideal. Most flights are not sold out and, normally, we can easily re-seat a

customer who prefers not to sit in this location. However, the Dec. 21 flight was completely full, and we have apologized to the customer who wrote to us about the concerns. If there was a quick and easy solution to this problem, we would do it in a whiz. However, the aircraft configuration is fixed and there is little we can do at this point to just flush away the issue.

So what have we learned from this tawdry business? That airline seating is something of a lottery, where the only prize is a vile smell, and that the companies profiting from our discomfort think it's all rather funny. Which it is, fairly. As long as it's not happening to you.

The 10 most dangerous holiday destinations in the world (3 of which you might even accidentally visit, if you don't read this)

Why anyone bothers to publish an annual list of the ten worst holiday destinations in the world is something of a mystery. We've already established that you can have an awful time just about anywhere and, on perusing the list below, you might well agree with me that, if people are silly enough to consider holidaying in most of these places, then, quite honestly, the gene pool is a better place without them. Still. The list exists and it would be remiss of me not to mention it.

1 Afghanistan

Rather an obvious one at the top of the list. Almost entirely lawless and populated exclusively, it seems, by short-tempered Mujahadeen, unscrupulous heroin traders and trigger-happy American military personnel. It's also more or less carpeted with landmines and there isn't even a Center Parcs. Quite the hard sell for your high street travel agent.

2 Somalia

Another no-brainer, I would suggest. At least Somalia has more picturesque hazards to excite the reckless tourist, though, with pirates and warlords providing the main attractions. Somalians, like Afghans and pretty much everyone else on this list, also absolutely *loathe* anyone who looks European and there really isn't much that the Commission for Racial Equality can do about it.

3 Iraq

Well, really. I don't need to tell you about this one, do I? There are numerous reported cases of Bird Flu in the northern part of the country for a start. Worth risking for the ancient monuments, perhaps?

4 Zimbabwe

A country in more or less constant political collapse, with runaway inflation and one of the most corrupt police forces ever established. Very pretty countryside, though, apparently.

5 Colombia

A country so rich in natural resources – oil fields, gold, silver, emeralds, platinum, cocaine and coal – is a country worth fighting over. So that's what the Colombians have been doing pretty much since records began. Optimistic backpackers straying into Colombia hoping to sample its most famous export are often surprised to discover that it has the highest murder rate per capita and the highest kidnapping rate per capita worldwide. It's nice to be best at something, isn't it?

6 Haiti

A beautiful tropical Caribbean island best known for its colourful Voodoo tradition. Your friends and workmates will be thrilled to get a postcard from Haiti, because it will mean you haven't been kidnapped, murdered or turned into a zombie. Yet.

7 Democratic Republic of Congo

Currently teetering on the brink of a bloody revolution, the Democratic Republic of Congo (the unstable and trigger-happy Congolese government are *especially* keen that you remember the 'Democratic' part) shows every sign of improving on the 1,000 people who die every day from disease (including a huge AIDS epidemic) and hunger by adding a brutal civil war into the mix.

8 Mexico

A surprise top ten placing for the perennial tourist favourite. Challenging Colombia in the per capita violent death stakes, Mexico is a primary conduit for the pan-American drugs trade with all the concomitant armed gangs one might expect. A friendly, industrious and enterprising people, Mexicans will just as soon turn their hand to carjacking and kidnap as cocaine trafficking.

9 Pakistan

A destination that appeals mostly to UK residents with family ties in the area, which is probably just as well. There is a healthy variety of Al Qaeda-sponsored terrorist groups in Pakistan, with each one hating Westerners more than the preceding one, so, if you look even a teensy bit British, the locals will be falling over themselves to kidnap you or blow you up. Absolutely *delicious* food, though, if you live long enough to eat it.

10 Thailand

One of the most popular long-haul destinations, and one of the most dangerous if you venture on to the roads. Whereas you're less likely to be *deliberately* harmed than in some of the other places we've discussed, visitors venturing out of their hotels will still probably need to claim on their travel insurance at some point. Over 17,000 people are killed every year in traffic accidents on (or near) Thailand's roads. Drunk driving is more or less the standard and hailing a taxi is – given that the regulations governing who is or isn't a taxi driver are rather elastic – a distinctly bold decision.

Appendix: The UN's Top 5 hit travel trouble spots by category.

Murders per capital – 1: Colombia 2: South Africa 3: Jamaica 4: Venezuela 5: Russia

Kidnappings per capita – 1: Colombia 2: Mexico 3: Philippines 4: Ecuador 5: Venezuela

Rape victims – 1: New Zealand 2: Austria 3: Finland 4: Sweden 5: Australia

Total crimes per capita – 1: Dominica 2: New Zealand 3: Finland 4: Denmark 5: Chile

Total prisoners – 1: United States 2: China 3: Russia 4: India 5: Brazil

Total robberies – 1: Spain 2: US 3: Mexico 4: South Africa 5: Russia

Assault victims – 1: Saint Kitts 2: United Kingdom! Yay! 3: New Zealand 4: Australia 5: Canada

The Rucksack Raj: Backpacking through the Third World

During the golden age of the British Empire, the right sort of British family would ship off their dimmer children to assorted colonies as soon as they had finished their education so that they could patronise poorer, browner people and build railways etc. for them.

Despite the regrettable loss of nearly all of our Crown dominions, we still do much the same sort of thing today: fewer large-scale infrastructure projects are undertaken, and a great deal more silly hats are purchased, but just as many people are insulted and patronised, so the whole system still works almost as well.

Recent figures suggest that over 70 per cent of the email traffic in the world is spam. Almost all the rest is sent from Internet cafés in Kathmandu by gap-year students who need some more money and clean socks. There's more to travelling the world in your gap year than ostentatiously waving your digital camera at starving Brazilian street children or asking a Malawian subsistence farmer if he has a spare iPod charger, though. Many students lend a helping hand in local schools while they are travelling. For example, Prince William briefly did some teaching in a school in Chile and taught his pupils some valuable stuff about wombats that I am sure will come in handy should any of them ever find themselves in Australia. Following our future monarch's lead, an increasing number of British students are volunteering to travel thousands of miles to deprived communities in order to share their valuable knowledge and skills. The fact that each generation of British students is even less well-educated than the preceding one and that a Media Studies qualification may not be the *most* useful asset in a rain forest does not deter these intrepid individuals from lecturing hutfuls of rapt but shoeless Tanzanian schoolchildren about Hegel, semiotics and *chiaroscuro*, of course.

Still, they're only there for a year and the kids will soon forget that they've had their time wasted by a well-fed white person with an iPod, so there's no lasting harm done, while the Gap Year Colonialist is sure to bring home a slightly holier-than-thou attitude and some terrible ethnic clothes that, with care, will last a lifetime.

Jet lag*: God's way of keeping you in your place

Although recent reports suggest that the endlessly re-cycled air in aeroplanes may be at least partly to blame, jet lag is still considered by most people to be the result of moving from one's designated position on the globe too quickly for the body clock to acclimatise to the change in longitude. You can, of course, minimize the effects of jet lag by picking holiday resorts that are on the same merid-ian as your home, but for us Brits that equates to a choice of Spain, Burkina Faso or the Antarctic. Most people

---

* Male readers should consider this section optional. You'll still get jet lag, but you probably won't notice. Not with that pretty little travel com-pany rep running around in a bikini all fortnight.

choose to pick destinations in more interesting destinations with fewer military coups per week and risk the dehydration, nausea, loss of appetite, disorientation, irritability and mild depression that are, of course, an essential part of any foreign holiday but will be exacerbated by high-speed air travel.

Jet lag does not visit its full ruinous power on all travellers equally. Women and the under 30s are particularly prone. Those women who have any *children* that are under 30 are probably best off planning a week in Antarctica because *he*'ll be no help – not with that half-dressed holiday rep flitting round. Trollop. *She*'s no better than she should be . . .

There are numerous remedies suggested to at least minimise jet lag's deleterious effects – shining a bright light on your knees, which presumably functions by refocusing the husband's attention back on to your legs and away from that slutty rep; Viagra, which I assume is a more direct approach – after all, you're pretty much obliged to stay in bed for a while if your husband's laid up with the Shepard's Sundial; or buying a watch that speeds up or slows down automatically according to your location. These last options are paralysingly expensive and are really only any use of you're travelling constantly, for example, if you're an airline pilot, but then you might need to know the actual time for reasons of navigation and, with one of those Micky Mouse jet lag timepieces, you're in mortal peril of reversing your Boeing into a mountain, crushing the poor sod in seat 29E.

The final recommended remedy is to avoid drinking alcohol for the entirety of the flight and a few days either side. Words rather fail me here. If you can't have a gin and tonic in a sharp-rimmed plastic cup at 65,000 feet, where can you have one? It's one of the few pleasures of going anywhere.

Here's a suggestion that might help: forget the plane tickets. Spend the money on extra gin instead. Send the kids to your mother's. Draw the curtains for two weeks so you can't see where the sun is anyway. Now that's a holiday. Might as well hang on to that Viagra, though. You never know . . .

Continental lager, and other treacheries

You'll probably plan to go on holiday somewhere warm, which means you'll get thirsty, which means you'll want to drink a fair bit, and you won't have any work to do the next day, so it might as well be beer, because beer is delicious and refreshing and feels a great deal more grown-up than cherryade. Equally, with the world's climate in turmoil (principally because the US refuses to sign up to the Kyoto accords and China seems to be building power stations quicker than we can build . . . well *anything*), the place that looked so warm in the brochure* is probably snowbound from July to September now and so you'll be holed up in a draughty wooden chalet feeling like Captain Scott, which means you'll want to drink a fair bit to warm yourself up, and you won't have any work to do even if you could dig yourself out of the snowdrift, so it might as well be beer, because beer is delicious and refreshing and feels more grown-up than a sachet of hot chocolate.

Now, the thing about the beer they sell in popular holiday hangouts like France and Spain is this: it comes in those funny little bottles, so one is never enough. And if you've had two, you might as well pop open a third – you're on holiday, after all – by which time your critical faculties will be impaired and so one more makes six and then you can probably have another one if you have something to eat first, but you've got some cashews, so you can have another one and . . . is that nine now? Or ten? If you can't remember, you'll have to start again, so that's definitely two: it doesn't taste like much, so it can't be strong and, oh, look, doesn't the ceiling look funny from down here.

* Brochure photographs always look like they were taken in the 1970s, don't they? It's something about the slightly yellow-tinged colour space, I think. Is that because tour operators want to subliminally remind us of those endless summer holidays of our youth? Or because the pictures really *were* taken in the 1970s, because that's the last available photo before the hotel started falling down as a result of the biblical torrent of rain that's been pouring down it ever since Kajagoogoo were number one?

You won't be the first person repatriated by your travel insurance provider with kidney failure, let me assure you.

24 hours on a coach

No matter how hard we work, or how handsomely remunerated we may be for our efforts, nearly all of us have to make a few economies now and then. (No, of course I don't mean you, Ma'am! And may I say how radiant you're looking on those new 1st class stamps?) One possible belt-tightening tactic is to travel by coach. Neither as fast as an aeroplane, nor as comfortable as a train, and lacking the flexibility of schedule one might achieve if driving oneself, the coach is one step above the bicycle in the pecking order of holiday conveyance.

Travelling any greater distance than, say, from a school to an inter-school rugby fixture a couple of miles away involves a good deal of making of packed lunches, which are scientifically designed to leave you sated and adequately hydrated without necessitating a trip to the tiny and malodorous onboard chemical toilet, which would result in mere shame for an adult coach passenger but, for a teenage tourist, lasting mortification of the kind that traditionally precipitates an extended bout of self-harm.

In an irony that will not be lost on readers of this book, it's teenage trekkers who most commonly have the freedom to go on holiday while lacking the financial resources to travel in any degree of style. Consequently, holiday coaches are generally packed to the gunwales with the under 20s. While a few more boisterous passengers will run amok at the back of the coach, sparking up a menthol and drinking warm lager on the outbound trip and boasting about their love bites and vomiting on the return leg, more sensitive souls will be brushing their hair out of their eyes a lot and reading an improving paperback while trying not to think about the mounting pressure in their abdomen.

It killed Tycho Brahe, you know.

Passport photos: Why they make you look like a criminal

With virtually every UK citizen owning a digital camera, or a mobile phone that thinks it's a digital camera, and image editing software so ubiquitous it's essentially free, there's no excuse not to have at least one good photograph of yourself any more.

You've got at least one bad photo of yourself, though, haven't you?

It's in that little red book you only look at once a year. With a five-year-old hairstyle and a haunted expression that bespeaks the existential anxiety in the mind of every passport owner: orange curtain? blue curtain? just plain white? Which one will make you look least like an ex-IRA gunrunner? The worry alone will be enough to derail any sense of composure you managed to pull together as you packed yourself into the tiny booth and fiddled with the peculiar rotating stool until at least the majority of your head was dimly reflected in the sinister-looking bullet-proof glass. There are a multiplicity of options that the kind people at Photo-Me International plc have to offer you: amusing digital 'wigs', droll slogans, sappy graphics, but no one chooses *them*. They want the standard mug-shot, please, and to be on their way without too much humiliating delay. Photo-Me probably think all those options will appeal to teenagers, but they seem to have forgotten that every single teenager in the Western world has a mobile phone full of amusing photographs of them-selves and their friends (plus a few rather comical videos showing those same friends committing common assault) and the computer expertise to add as many Care Bears and cartoon pirates to the images as they wish before posting them on MySpace for the edification of sinister perverts who will groom them like so many My Little Ponies.

All the multifarious options serve to do nothing but compound the curtain/no curtain dilemma and leave the hapless passport applicant in a technological pickle that is unlikely to subside before the long-anticipated flash catches them by surprise and immortalises them in a pose of unalloyed terror. That wait outside the booth as the (unconscionably long, given the technology available) development process proceeds is typified by some artful manoeuvres as the photographic subject calculates every possible sightline to ensure that no passing stranger catches sight of the humiliating likeness before it can be snatched from the little slot with the mysterious hairdryer in it and concealed in the first available pocket.

The ghastly image must then be witnessed by a local Alderman, Ratcatcher or Lamplighter before being sent off to a distant government agency, where everyone will have a good laugh before repairing to the pub for lunch and then come back to the office a little worse for wear and lose your photo, obliging you to go through the whole debilitating experience again. There's a science behind this humiliating process, though: after these extended tribulations, you'll look almost exactly as tired and bedraggled as you might after a couple of hours on an overbooked tourist flight, making the job of the thoroughly bored functionary who has to check these things a little easier.

THINGS YOU CAN ONLY DO @ HOME #10:
Listen to the wireless

When you want a bit of low-intensity entertainment, the kind you don't need to participate in *too* actively because you're piloting a half-hundredweight lump of rented metal along an *autostrada* at 100 kph or sucking down a frosty *Dos Equis* in a hammock, what you need is a nice bit of radio. Now, here in Britain we've done something rather clever: we've all clubbed together and bought ourselves some radio stations that bang out top quality content at pretty much every hour of the day. As a result, our commercial stations are driven by something other than the vile grasp of Mammon, because they feel obliged, just out of pride, really, to put up a show that's at least halfway competitive with the mighty BBC.

Not so elsewhere in the world. I know it's not fashionable to say so now we live under the dogmatic tyranny of BBC-engendered political correctness, but foreigners can't do radio for toffee. French radio is a case in point. You wander up and down the dial hopefully while steering with one hand and keeping a wary eye on the Gallic maniacs who seem to think that having fallen in the magic potion as a baby makes them immune to car accidents and you hear the dying bars of something cool. Some Earth Wind and Fire usually, I find. Then some lunatic shouts 'Radio Maximum!' and gabbles away in some godforsaken excuse for a language, but you think you'll give it a couple of minutes and there's bound to be something decent on next – maybe Sly and the Family Stone is a wish too far, but at least some Take That or Thin Lizzy. Instead you'll be expected to endure twenty-five minutes of Johnny' alliday punctuated by baffling mile-a-minute advertisements for garlic, or cheese, or white flags or whatever it is that French people buy.

The impression seems to be, at least from my point of view, that there's little care involved in the creation of foreign radio. Their airwaves seem like an empty embarrassment that has to be filled with something, anything, as quickly and cheaply as possible and, if that means dropping the needle on some old Sylvie Vartan tunes, then so be it, whereas, in Britain, we have teams of smart young men grinding out the *bons mots* like so many amusing peppercorns from a vast phallic (metaphorical) peppermill made of funny. These chaps are, of course (quite rightly), being handsomely remunerated from the public purse for each droll remark.

Now, there's no *News Quiz* on French radio. There's not even a *Now Show*. I have no idea what the French (or the Spanish or the Italians, for that matter) do with their bright young men, but they certainly aren't giving them jobs writing topical sketch shows for national speech-based radio stations. If you're planning on doing any driving, ironing or general slacking about in your holiday fortnight, therefore, make you sure you do it somewhere that gets Radio 2, at the very least.

TRAVEL TIPS #6:
EUROPE – Faliraki – What it is and how to avoid it

If you can add your age to your IQ and still come up with less than 100, you'll probably quite like Faliraki: unless, that is, you're just a pleasant middle-aged teetotaller who mainly listens to things like *The News Quiz* on Radio 4 but didn't do very well in maths at school. Faliraki is a resort composed almost entirely of theme pubs, many with their own unique character. Some focus principally on lasting liver damage, others offer fight-based entertainment, most, though, offer both of the above blended with a non-stop parade of ill-advised sexual hi-jinks which are filmed by Sky TV for the entertainment of people who weren't there, or can't remember if they were or not.

Because package deals to the land of the vomit-carpeted Greek resort are so cheap, it's possible for almost anyone, no matter what their income, to visit Faliraki and see at first hand the picturesque local customs, like chunky Middlesbrough shopgirls dancing on bar tables that are ill equipped to support them, or comparatively bright young women with a promising political future but an astonishing lack of foresight flashing their sunburned tits at a Sky camera crew. Every night ends up with the traditional crop-haired car mechanic brawl or, on feast days, a shirtlessly lanky pizza delivery executive retching convulsively into the gutter.

Every single indiscretion, injury and life-threatening condom decision is captured on a multiplicity of red-eyed cameraphone pictures and placed on the Internet, of course, where it will remain in perpetuity, so even if you do somehow graduate from riding a moped for Dominos to a position of authority in the legal profession your mistakes will be displayed online for all to see until the end of time. What starts with a sip of sambucca will end with a spread in the Sunday papers. You could always just not bother. It's your choice.

The espadrille and 5 other holiday shopping mistakes

It seems that, wherever you decide to go on holiday, from the Andes to the Arctic, there will be some optimistic soul trying to sell you espadrilles. These deeply unflattering and impractical shoes, originally of Catalan origin, have a flat rope sole that, while offering no appreciable support, will hold virtually limitless quantities of rain or seawater against the foot, making use on the beach or in a sudden shower marginally less pleasant than a protracted session of Bastinado. Irritatingly, these cripplingly uncomfortable fashion mistakes will hold together just long enough to be an additional challenge when re-packing your suitcase (and then perhaps one or two amusing enquiries about your membership of Wham if you risk them down your local), before unravelling and wriggling down to the sea, to swim back to the ramshackle stall where you bought them so they can be sold to some other improvident shopper.

Second only to the espadrille, and generally sold from the same commercially unsound emporia, is the holiday straw hat. Available in the gentleman's or lady's version, this item will not only, of course, defy the dimensions of any known suitcase, but will also infect every holiday photo with a jaunty comedy, which can only detract from the dignity of the subject or, indeed, from the majesty of any pyramids in front of which he or she poses. What seems like a light-hearted if practical purchase on holiday becomes a photographically immortalised testament to your poor judgement in millinery that will be commented upon and chuckled over in perpetuity by everyone with five spare minutes and a copy of Internet Explorer.

Another classic headgear mistake is the woolly breast with earflaps. Knitted by poorly treated orphans in Chinese sweatshops, then transported halfway across the world in carbon-spewing tankers for the edification of self-consciously worthy vegetarians from the Home Counties backpacking in Peru, who will then fly them a quarter of the way back, to be worn as a gap year badge of honour, the woolly breast is an horrific insult to fashion that looks (if this were at all possible) even more ludicrous in the Glastonbury downpour than it does when the wearer is perched proudly atop a festering pile of tourist litter in Machu Picchu.

The holiday T-shirt is conspicuous consumption writ large. It's supposed to say 'I want to shout about how much money I can afford to spend on holidays' but it actually says 'At 50 lira for a gossamer-thin garment that won't survive a 40 degree wash, that Turkish stallholder saw me coming'. As a souvenir gift for the stay-at-home relative, it attests to the buyer's lack of imagination far more than it bespeaks his desire to spread vacation joy.

Ethnic knick-knacks and ornaments levy a terrible price on the home they end up in. The *Nimba* mask may signify fertility to the peoples of Sub-Saharan Africa, but it represents a major interior design/family politics crisis to your sister-in-law with the minimalist décor aspirations and the *Livingetc* subscription and, candidly, it means bugger all to the Chinese sweatshop slave who actually made it.

Finally, if you buy olive oil, a curious local liqueur or, for that matter, anything in a bottle, you will *never* be able to get the smell, or the splinters of glass, out of your nice summer shirt.

THINGS YOU CAN ONLY DO @ HOME #11:
Being a whatever-tarian

Although being intolerant of other nationalities is, these days, somewhat frowned upon in polite society, being intolerant of one foodstuff or another is considered more or less de rigueur. More and more British people, it seems, are becoming vegetarians in order to improve their health, to preserve the environment or to impress teenage girls. Indeed, vegetarianism is so firmly established now in

British culture that maverick spirits are constantly looking for newer, more extreme dietary disciplines in order to better distinguish themselves as culinary aesthetes. Nowadays, no dinner party is complete without someone dropping a purifying tablet into the mineral water and inquiring of the hostess whether the vol-au-vents were prepared in a nut-free environment or if the cocaine is fair trade.

The dietary philosophy du jour seems to be that one should only consume foods that could be found within one's natural environment. Not so bad for me, with a Chinese takeaway and a kebab shop both within a short walk of my home, but something of a trial for the Bushmen of the Kalahari – for whom, I am reliably assured, the endless suppers of roast eland with a wild berry *jus* are quite beginning to pall. Which is why the vegetarian lifestyle has been so enthusiastically taken up in the UK, with its plentiful sources of varied and nutritious food, but is still comparatively rare elsewhere in Europe.

As Britons we may be decreasingly tolerant of gluten (whatever that is), but our legendary tolerance for alternative lifestyles* remains undiminished. Conversely, in

* If someone should express a preference for a handful of kapok over a nourishing breakfast of Crunchy Nut Cornflakes anointed with Baileys, then we will politely avert our eyes and let them make their own mistakes. Should they go on to order some in a British restaurant, the unflappable maitre d' will glide into the kitchen and slaughter a stuffed bear without batting an eyelash. That's what makes British restaurants the best in the world. If you can find one.

many European and American holiday destinations, vegetarian holidaymakers can doggedly explain their perversion a thousand times using an ingenious combination of phrasebook, mime and pictionary, but the vegetarian pasta sludge that they will eventually, grudgingly, be provided with will inevitably be topped off with a few generous handfuls of chopped ham.

If you have, for whatever reason, espoused an exotic food fad or affected one of the more fashionable allergies, you will still be treated almost as if you were a normal person in Britain, but overseas you will struggle to describe your culinary requirements, which will be as alien to the famously omnivorous Continentals as the consumption of a garden gastropod is to all decent people.

Losing your game face

Here's something you wouldn't necessarily expect in a humorous collection of loosely travel-related essays: I'm going to explain how evolution works. When the lioness* stalks a herd of gazelle (or eland, they taste pretty much the same, to a lion) across the Serengeti, she doesn't just pick one out at random. There is an aura around every

---

* There's no point letting the male lion do the shopping. He'll just come back with something ridiculously impractical, like an elephant.

living thing that reveals its health, fitness and general *weltanschauung*. Don't worry, I'm not going all new age on you here. That's not the kind of chap I am. I am assured by 'experts' on the 'Internet' that this is a field that can be readily photographed with suitable lighting (the name I expect you're trying to remember right now is Semyon Kirlian), and can even be perceived by the human eye under certain special circumstances. Of course, I have no reason to doubt the collective wisdom of every crackpot on the Internet and I'm sure the majestic lion believes them too. Whether the lioness sees these putative auras consciously or perceives them in the same subliminal way that I believe we do, I wouldn't like to say, but she certainly takes cues as to which one of the herd is most likely to come along quietly and not require her to burn up any more energy in the chase than is absolutely necessary. The usefulness of this occult information source is the true engine behind those millions of tons of pollution dumped into the earth's atmosphere every year in the name of business travel. No matter how many telephones, emails and webcams we have, there's something about meeting someone face to face that is just irreplaceable.

Even though, in the UK, the intervention of medical and social welfare agencies has effectively banished evolution to the history books (where many Americans would be shocked to find it), the subliminal clues about our state of readiness are still used by muggers and their close relatives, corporate raiders, when it comes to selecting a target. Two weeks in a hammock reading the latest Paulo Coelho will weaken that carefully contrived carapace of street smarts you've nurtured since secondary school and, on your return to the UK – whether you live in Moss Side or Mayfair – you'll be marked out to urban predators as the weakest wildebeest in the herd.

In Paris they *kiss* on main street? The iniquities of alfresco micturition

In the UK we bask in the comforting glow of closer surveillance than any society outside the febrile world of Phillip K. Dick's paranoid science fiction dreams. When you add in the number of foot patrols still undertaken by old-fashioned bobbies, which is supplemented by occasional peregrinations by the new kind of pretend bobbies that are effectively special forces traffic wardens but will still issue you with a voucher for a clip round the ear if you misbehave, you have an environment wherein repairing to a convenient alley to shoot a little pool after a night of refreshing cold drinks is an increasingly inadvisable option. Furthermore, Britain's enviably damp climate ensures that the occasional tipsy micturitions of late night revellers so heroically refreshed that they momentarily forget the ever-watchful electronic eyes of our political masters are soon washed away by a welcome downpour.

You will doubtless be unsurprised to hear that this agreeably urine-free state of affairs does not prevail elsewhere in the world. A mixture of laissez-faire law enforcement, a casual approach to public nudity and an unacceptably arid climate lend many popular holiday spots a noisome odour that has not been experienced in Britain since the last alchemists gave up trying to make phosphorous out of tramp's wee. If you follow the instructions for city walks off the beaten track in Barcelona that are touted in other, lesser, guide books, you will find yourself at the heart of the vilest miasma of urine stench since Hercules cleaned out the Augean stables.

We must concede that many of these open-air urinators may, indeed, be wayward British youths giddy with new-found freedom, but the lesson that should be taken from that fact is that, taken out of our Motherland, we can soon lapse into sloppy Continental habits and that, for that reason alone, we are best off staying where the firm but caring agents of British law can be on hand to guide us back on to the correct, dry path.

Skis, snowboards and other instruments of torture

There's a high price to pay for the transitory thrill of hurtling down a snowy hill at 60 mph without the benefit of an airbag or side impact protection system. Contrary to the popular image of the novice skier being wheeled through customs with a broken leg, the most common skiing injury is tearing your thumb half off with your ski pole. Actions as diverse as adjusting the browning level knob on your toaster, buttering some toast or opening a jar of marmalade are well-nigh impossible without the use of your thumbs. Gentleman skiers might also be disappointed to discover that the homespun comfort of self-abuse is a closed book to the thumbless invalid, and, basically, if you can't shuffle around the house in your dressing gown eating toast and having the occasional *ménage à une* when you're off sick with a skiing injury, there's pretty much no point even paying for all that expensive travel, tuition and equipment hire anyway.

Snowboarding, skiing's more modish cousin, is easier on the thumbs, but, if anything, more ruinous to the ankle, which makes even the simple act of trotting downstairs to have breakfast and watch *Trisha* an excruciatingly painful experience. When you factor in the very real danger of falling in with a bunch of relentlessly matey IT support engineers from Harrogate while you're on the slopes, snowboarding is simply too hazardous an undertaking to be considered.

Despite the certainty of injury and a miserable toast and masturbation-free convalescence, skiing and snowboarding are, astoundingly, about the *least* insane of the 'extreme' holiday activities. The fact that your first day on a kayaking vacation will be learning how to drown means that we need not detain ourselves too long in discussion of such a wilfully suicidal pastime. Only mountain climbing, with its inevitable hazardous rescue made at the taxpayer's expense, is a more recklessly self-flagellating activity.

Extreme sports holidaymakers penalise not only themselves but every other traveller by driving up insurance premiums with their routine, almost inevitable requirement for emergency medical repatriation. Even if they didn't annoy everyone they encountered by clunking them in the knees with the awkward unwieldy impedimenta of their chosen activity on the train, the insurance thing would be enough to make pariahs of them all. By all means sacrifice your financial and physical well-being on the specious altar of the adrenalin rush, if you feel the need, just don't expect any of us to sign your cast.

You'll miss it when it's not there: Marmite

There are certain British institutions so fundamentally woven into the fabric of our national life that we occasionally forget that other countries don't have them too. Radio 4's *Today* programme, for example: it's easy to assume that people all over the world wake up to James Naughtie doggedly asking a greasy politician the same question over and over again while the Westminster weasel trots out the same non-committal anodyne sound-byte until everyone in the country wants to rise up as one and behead the entire government, but then everyone realises at about the same time that they can't do that because it would make them late for work and so they just have a calming cup of tea and a bit of thoughtful toast instead. You'll also be shocked to hear, just to name one example, that the former republic of Yugoslavia (now known, I believe, as Prince) doesn't have such an institution. Which is a shame, really – perhaps, if they *did* have their own high quality early morning news and current affairs radio programme, they wouldn't have gone through all that unpleasantness in the 1990s.

Another thing that no one seems to have is Marmite. Easily overlooked, you might think. However, should you find yourself on a clubbing holiday in Ibiza or the like, you may be tempted to consider a judicious amount of Ecstasy as part of your evening's refreshment. It certainly enables one to stay up a little later than usual, thereby extracting maximum value from one's club admission fee. It also fosters a rather congenial mood, leading, as often as not, to an inconclusive but nevertheless thoroughly agreeable sexual coupling.

Of course, with Ecstasy, as with most other intoxicants, you are effectively taking out an overdraft on pleasures you might reasonably experience spread over an indeterminate period in the future, so one rather festive night of intense amusement must be paid for with something of a trial when it comes to getting up the next morning. Or, as like as not, the next afternoon.

The only proven method to restore one's equilibrium after a night of such illicit refreshments is a substantial round of white bread toast topped off with Marmite. You may plead with Spanish room service staff in vain; you can even send one of your party to prowl the *supermercado* like some shambling rave comedown zombie, but Marmite will not be forthcoming. Without the black panacea, your pleasure overdraft repayments will be protracted and painful, with no Carol Vorderman to group them into one manageable monthly payment. I accept that, in polite circles, the consumption of Ecstasy tablets is now considered rather passé and this discussion might be considered moot, but I would ask those elite tastemakers and disco glitterati reading this to remember that caravans aren't exactly cutting edge, and some people seem to enjoy those on holiday too.

Ticket prices: The ultimate insult

Everyone knows that holidays are more expensive when the kids are off school, yet no one can quite explain why. Certainly there's no significant seasonal variability in the price of aviation fuel or the remuneration packages of chambermaids. When pressed, tour operators make airy generalisations about 'supply and demand', but what they're really saying is 'You don't have a choice, so just pay up'. Interestingly, while it's more expensive to fly to the Bahamas in the summer, a different type of petrol must be used to get people to popular ski resorts, because the pricing for trips to (for example) Zermatt becomes markedly more eye-watering in January. It's hard to find another industry that so blatantly gouges extra profit out of its customers on such an entirely arbitrary basis. Even McDonalds, the woolly liberal's favourite corporate whipping boy, charges the same for a Big Mac in high summer as it does in the peak 'staggering out of office party a little the worse for wear' season. Face it: the airlines are laughing at you.

Surf's up, fatty

The travel business is not the only shadowy conspiracy that's trying to ruin all your fun. As recently as the 1950s, women were allowed to eat as many cakes as they liked and sort out any excess bulges with well-engineered corsetry. The thing is, once someone's bought a good corset, they don't particularly need a second one, whereas the assorted quack nostrums, fanciful books and cardboard-flavoured non-foods of the diet industry represent an endlessly replenished revenue stream to Illuminati Health SA, a wholly owned division of Bilderberg Diet Plans PLC. So it was that the tyranny of bony self-hatred was visited on our womenfolk, and we stood by and said nothing.

Then, in the last few years, the beast turned its gaze upon us men. Until as recently as the 1980s, a certain softness around the equator bespoke a gentleman who had arrived and could afford some of the finer things in life, like regular pub lunches and those special trousers with a really long zip. It could have remained thus in perpetuity, but for a small cadre of gender traitors who transformed the meaning of the phrase 'six pack' from a refreshing accompaniment to a barbecue to the sort of abdomen you can grate parmesan on.

As a consequence, the purchase of swimwear for the average kind of gentleman is no longer a case of selecting a Speedo small enough to fit underneath the prosperous dome of his paunch and, instead, has become a Kafkaesque trial involving visits to an endless parade of ever-more humiliating surf shops staffed by snake-hipped teenagers who spend their meagre stipend on piercings and tattoos rather than getting a good Beef Wellington down them.

When the kind of hard-working gentleman who's actually keeping this great nation's economy going by sacrificing his health to gruelling sedentary work eventually gets to the beach, he will encounter legions of *flâneurs* who are content to spend their time in (government subsidised, I don't doubt) gyms lifting serious iron. The rest of us don't even lift a heavy book until we're already at the beach, and by then it's too late.

The irony, of course, is that what every decent chap really wants to do with his holiday is spend a fortnight in his shed assembling balsa–wood aircraft until he is so giddy with dope fumes he starts seeing tiny M. C. Escher lizards on his workbench. He only goes on holiday to please the memsahib and she's just as miserable on the beach in her ill-fitting bikini as he is in those ridiculous calf-length shorts he was eventually pressured into buying. Why is he wearing them? He hasn't got a surf-board. He hasn't even touched an ironing board since the late 1980s. Which is about the last time he saw his feet, now you mention it . . .

And you thought I was making all this up: The research trip

Let it not be said that this book is composed *entirely* of barely-thought-through opinions. Even if that should ultimately prove to be the case, I made personal sacrifices in order to essay some research to ensure that you, dear reader, are furnished with the fullest account of the iniquities of the travel business.

Easter weekend on the Costa Blanca might seem, at first blush, a pleasant sojourn in balmy temperatures with the bonuses of some rather laissez-faire licensing laws and the occasional picturesque procession involving tipsy but devout locals wearing tastefully pastel Ku Klux Klan drag and carrying a frankly rather Tarantinoesque crucifix.

The very idea.

Every day was a washout, which might be testing enough with an all-adult party, but the addition of an easily bored four-year-old to the mix created an entertainment conundrum of biblical proportions. Demonstrating that I was very much a tourist, with no pretensions to being a 'traveller', I threw myself upon the gentle mercies of the knowledgeable if surly young lady in the local Tourist Office. The answer was, she assured me, readily at hand: the circus was in town.

Now you may, when you imagine a circus, imagine the kind of affair we used to put on in the UK before it went all Chinese dragons and Cirque de Soleil. Professional entertainers with a pragmatically businesslike, rather than genuinely tender, concern for their animal charges, for example, performing in a sawdust arena encircled by a stout fence and some reassuringly sturdy tiered seating.

What you might not expect to see is a loosely sprinkled oval of sand with a couple of lawn chairs dotted haphazardly around its circumference and no physical barrier between the entertainers and the (and these inverted commas are there for a reason) 'entertained'. Mindful as I was of the Tourist Office lady's parting recommendation of the circus as having the finest lion tamer in all Europe, it was with no small sense of trepidation that I took my seat on the fringes of the gladiatorial arena. I positioned myself as near as seemed polite to the sole exit and eyed the handful of other patrons to assess which ones might best serve as a barrier between my firstborn and any hungry lions that might be on the bill.

The Spanish take on entertainment-based animal husbandry is rather different to what you may have seen in the UK. An assortment of animals (a camel, a llama, two different kinds of bull) were paraded around the ring and whipped enthusiastically and constantly by the unshaven man in greasy Levis and a threadbare ringmaster's jacket while I wondered whether my early exit might be considered an insult by the rather substantial gentleman with an impressive collection of tattoos who had taken my money and now stood by the exit of the tent with what seemed to me a rather pointed expression. Anyway, the first four animals were just the warmup. Next on the agenda were two Shetland ponies, one of which had a rather terrified baboon strapped to its back. I am no wildlife expert, but whereas I am aware that, in baboons, a rather large and scarlet rear end is considered normal, even desirable, the vivid vermilion flesh of this particular example appeared to be painfully distended and wobbling about most unpleasantly, what with the larger Shetland's all-too-evident desire to get this monkey off its back. The smaller of the two ponies clearly thought something was awry too, because it kept sniffing the poor baboon's fundament in a most intrusively personal way. All the while, of course, the ringmaster was whipping the bejesus out of everything that moved. By this time I was resolved to leave, but was rather hampered by the fact that my lift home was not expected for a further twenty minutes, which meant that an early departure would consist of waiting outside this ramshackle tent in the middle of nowhere with a group of rather offended gypsy gentlemen. So I stayed put.

Next up was a clown who punched the ringmaster quite hard in the face in lieu of telling any jokes and was soon on his way. Then there was a balancing act that consisted of a rangy gentleman doing the same handstand over and over while a substantial young lady in a leotard laid on the floor quite near him. Time was nearly up. The finale was upon us. It had to be the lion, and based on what I had seen so far, it was unlikely to be a happy, gregarious lion. I subtly manoeuvred my child behind me and prepared for action.

The final act, though, was a man so weatherbeaten and tanned as to resemble a Pepperami in a wig. He emptied a black bin liner full of broken glass at the centre of the ring and rolled about on it for a bit. Then he stood, pulled a Zippo lighter from his jeans pocket and played the flame up and down his bare arms. The crackle of burning armpit hair was audible even over my child's inexplicable laughter. Of the advertised lion, there was no sign.

I have never been so happy to have been disappointed. The lesson here, if we can find one, is that, as bad as it can be to be a tourist abroad, to be an animal anywhere but here in the UK is ten times worse.

The treachery of the toenail

When did you last take a look at your toenails? Really *look* at them, I mean. What are they even *for*? They're useless as claws but we evolved them long before our toes needed to be defended against falling ratchet screwdrivers. They're not much use at that anyway. Anything more substantial than an Allen key and they'll crack like the lid on a crème caramel. They're probably a bit yellow, aren't they? And who can blame them? Stuck in sock or tights (depending on your gender/profession/predilections) for most of the year: they've got nothing better to do than succumb to mystery fungal infections.

But if you're taking your toenails on holiday – and most people do – you're going to be expected to wear sandals. Without socks, probably. So your toenail shame will be on show for all to see. Are you really going to add the price of a pedicure to the already ruinous expense of a holiday overseas? When you could have a perfectly nice time in your own back garden? With no one to look askance at your toes? It's a no-brainer when I put it like that, isn't it?

You're going skiing? Why not just drown a few kittens while you're at it?

To start with, you have two choices: either get a train to the airport and risk having some poor bugger's eye out with those pointy sticks, or drive. You might as well drive, you're going to be stinking up the great outdoors a lot more before *this* holiday's done. Then there's the plane, of course. Airline travel, apart from depleting the world's reserves of oil and peanuts to an insanely reckless degree, also squirts more pollutants into the delicate upper atmosphere than do the farts of every cow on the planet and the late Bernard Manning combined. That's true of every holiday to some joyless tourist trap, though. What makes skiing even more heinously stupid is the spiralling feedback loop of climate change insanity caused by artificial snow.

Because the world is, broadly speaking, becoming a hotter place*, there isn't as much snow as there used to

---

* Whether people believe that climate change is caused principally by the Industrial Revolution, solar temperature variation or God's wrath depends mainly on how much of an idiot they are. Whereas more than one factor may be in play here, you don't need Al Gore to tell you that releasing billions of tons of carbon dioxide into the atmosphere isn't the cleverest idea. It's like saying 'I'm not too sure why it's getting so warm in the car, so let's have a nice barbecue on the back seat while we think about it'.

be. This is a cause of quite some concern to the people who run ski resorts, dependent as they are on the vacation plans of minor royals and their hangers-on for the mortgage payments on those picturesque chalets that ski resort owners, by law, have to live in. So the resourceful resort people (who are all as Swiss as your *hat*) are making more snow. Not, as the tie-dyed idealists among you might be hoping, by using geological reiki to rebalance all of the negative *chi* or whatever it is that is caused by the thousands of jets ferrying braying public school simpletons to and fro between Sloane Square and Gstaad. The very idea. They're no more likely to do that than they are to clear up the tons of discarded batteries and sweet wrappers scattered all over the Matterhorn by dimwittedly solipsistic alpine holidaymakers.

No.

Instead they've set up massive snowmaking machines. These things suck in fuel and water with an appetite that would be comical, were it not so genocidally short-sighted, and spray out a nice covering of reasonably convincing imitation powder snow for the edification of posh people in sunglasses and puffa jackets. Remember puffa jackets? The really, really hilarious part about all this is that there isn't enough water in these areas to feed the snow makers because it's so warm. So it's flown in by helicopter.

Really.

So, on the one hand, you've got countries with thousands of heartbreakingly poor people dying, either through dehydration or wars over water rights, while, on the other hand, you've got a small elite of toffs, many of whom get their money from industries that generate pollution – as a (to be fair) necessary if unpleasant side-effect of the manufacture of products we all enjoy – causing even more dehydrating climate change *for a laugh*. Skiing isn't necessary. The last time anyone's life depended on skiing was in a James Bond film. And I'm pretty sure that wasn't even 100 per cent true.

10 things you really can't do anywhere hot

1 Be a Goth

The origins of the Goth aesthetic are not exactly lost in the mists of time. It was invented in a house in Bromley in the mid to late 1970s by a nice young girl called Susan who had a quiet afternoon and a job lot of black Dylon. Over the years, various additions and enhancements have been appended to the basic template. For example, in the 1960s and 1970s, you would occasionally see kids who had been born with one leg shorter than the other wearing a built up shoe. You don't seem to get them any more, but because many Goths seem to be afflicted with a modern variation of this condition, in which, tragically, *both* legs are too short to reach the ground, they wear *two* built up shoes. A bit like Herman Munster, only a touch funnier. The combination of the voluminous layers of black clothes that they wear, the pallid complexions that they tend (very sensibly) to exhibit, and the (to be frank) characteristic avoirdupois of the typical Goth conspire to make them unsuitable for tropical or even warm and temperate conditions and they should only be transported south by about 50 degrees of latitude – with extreme caution.

2 Mess around on the Internet

Logging on for five minutes to check your bank balance and then losing the entire evening to gardening your Facebook profile is one of the privileges that our forefathers sacrificed their very lives for us to enjoy. The thing is, after a couple of hours' use, computers tend to get a bit warm. Even those spiffy flat screens that everyone's got now can be a good deal more calescent than you'd expect. Sitting close to one for any period of time tends to impart a rosy glow, even if you're not perusing one of those 'one handed' websites. Just getting embroiled in a futile discussion about whether Mac users are LamerZ or not can raise your temperature by a degree or two. Even if you can miraculously attain access to the Internet while you're on holiday, and then miraculously wriggle out of being forced to go the inconveniently scheduled trip to the tiny town across the lake that looks exactly like the one you're staying in, you're still going to feel too warm to get any serious time wasting done. Then, when your other half comes back with a bottle of olive oil and some special liqueur that you really can't (with good reason) get anywhere else to find you sitting in front of the computer in just your vest and pants, you're going to have a lot of explaining to do. Now that's going to cool the atmosphere a bit.

3 Complain about the weather

'Should brighten up later', 'It was a bit blowy along the front', 'It pissed down all weekend' – these are the central planks of all British discourse. If we don't have them to act as the scaffolding from which all other dialogue is suspended, it's surprisingly hard to start a safe conversation at all. Make the neophyte mistake of asking someone about their house or their job and, within a couple of minutes, you're committing the unforgivable sin of asking them what they earn and the whole conversation will collapse like a verbal version of giant-size beer garden Jenga. Just as the Esquimaux have dozens of words for snow, so our great language is uniquely adapted for the drizzly conditions in which we are proud to make our home. The simple pleasure of a nice chat about nothing in particular is only available within a few dozen miles of where you're standing right now. Treasure it.

4 Go for a walk

If it's freezing out, and it rarely is, then, as long as you can bundle yourself up in coats and scarves and such, a walk can still be a pretty bracing and pleasurable affair. You can even justify stopping off at a convenient inn for a hot toddy or similar and it's not indulgence, it's *medicinal*. You can still more or less manage a walk if it's just warm, but if it's really genuinely hot (I mean Greece or Turkey hot here), you really can't go anywhere. It's too sunny to go outside without having long sleeves and trousers, otherwise you'll get sunburn (you can't rely on sunblock any more, it's illegal to even call it sunblock any more – it's now marketed as 'fly attractor'), but it's too hot to wear anything more than your glasses, so you have to stay indoors. Really, if you can't ankle around the park for half an hour and then slip into your local for a calming shandy, what's the point of being on holiday at all?

5 Have a DVD orgy

The Wire, *The Sopranos*, *Heroes*. Good modern television isn't meant to be enjoyed once a week like it was a bath or sex or something. The only way to really savour the majesty of a great television show is to blow £50 on a set of DVDs, draw the curtains, and curl up on your sofa with a loved one and a box of indifferent rosé. It's one of the most satisfying experiences of the twenty-first century. And you want to give that up to spend eight hours blistering in pitless sun while you're queuing for a look at the Colosseum? There's something wrong there . . .

6 Get heroically drunk

As long as you're an adult, and you don't have some debilitating medical condition, getting really drunk is great. Not just Friday evening drunk: I mean Christmas drunk, wedding drunk, the kind of drunk where you forget to have a glass of water before you go to bed and you wake up with toothpaste all over one cheek and Russell Brand's hair*. You can't just do it anywhere, though: if you've made the mistake of going on holiday somewhere really hot, and even if you *can* find your way back to your own bed in such unfamiliar surroundings, the benign early morning dehydration that merely sharpens one's appetite for a fry-up in our native land will, in toastier climes, pullulate into a vast interlinked series of unbearable aches and ailments which together might be described by the layman as a hangover but should more correctly be characterised as a near-death experience.

7 Skip a shower

Whether its through the quite correct desire to preserve our planet's dwindling resources, the pressure of our modern 24/7 lifestyle or just sheer pikeyness, we've all skipped a shower at some time or other. You can get away with it in Britain, most of the time. Even our hottest days are really only pleasantly mild and, as long as you avoid semaphore, no one need know that there's a great dark sweaty stain that smells like a tramp's duvet lurking in your armpit. Just try that in Miami, though. One careless scratch of the head and you'll clear Collins Avenue. Although, that might not be a bad thing.

* I've always had the impression that most members of The Cure do this on a daily basis.

8 Eat a proper pudding

All decent people like puddings. Proper puddings are best. Proper puddings have custard. Either the custard should be hot or the pudding (never both). As a consequence, you can no more enjoy a good hot apple crumble in Kos than you can force down a Solero in McMurdo Sound.

9 Drive

It's boiling. The car's a rental, so the aircon will either be broken or will be unbelievably fiddly and impossible to set just right, or more probably both. Everyone else will be driving on the wrong side of the road. There may well be children in the back who are whimpering about prickly heat. There will definitely be someone in the passenger seat who insists on using the map as a fan, so you'll be completely lost. All of the road signs will be erected on the assumption that not only do you speak Portuguese but that you've lived in Lisbon all your life and only need a few centimetres' notice for an important turning. Even if you do finally get to the poorly signposted beach you've been seeking for hours, you're bound to burn your incautiously exposed belly on the doorhandles when you're getting the towels off the back seat. Purgatory.

10 Be old

We're always reading about old people who carelessly frittered away too much of their youth fighting Nazis on our behalf and therefore failed to accumulate sufficient blankets to keep them warm in their twilight years, leading to death from hypothermia. What's less well known, but just as much of a killer, is the amount of old people who succumb to its opposite, hyperthermia. It's not just a problem for people lost in deserts; the Chicago heat wave of July 1995 caused more than 600 deaths in nine days. Most of those were the elderly, partly because they're physically weaker to start with, partly perhaps because they always seem to be wearing an overcoat. The death of Pheidippides, who ran the first marathon to bring the news of the Persian invasion to Athens, was almost certainly caused by heat stroke, and he was a fit young man in a sort of skirt. Just sitting in an inadequately air conditioned Greek hotel room can be enough to see off the only people who really *have* enough spare time for holidays. Especially if they insist on wearing a mac. If they hadn't gone on holiday, they could be sitting around contentedly in their own front rooms, with *Antiques Roadshow* to watch and a plentiful supply of biscuits that they've actually heard of. Which is all anyone wants really, in their twilight years.

Waiting for Raffles

Most people tend to take their holidays in July or August. Not Britain's doughty legion of burglars, though. August is their busy time. While you're away sunning yourself, the sedulous young men and women of the UK's petty crime industry are hard at work keeping insurers, locksmiths and pawn-shop owners in business.

In the frenetic rush to get out of the door with the requisite number of passports, tickets, credit cards etc., it's entirely natural for frazzled soon-to-be-holidaymakers to leave one set of keys hanging up just inside the front door. That small oversight and a fishing rod* is all your modern second-story man needs to gain access to your house and, quite possibly, the car parked outside too. For the more light-fingered consumer (and who knows, it could be you – books get pilfered too) August is Christmas. Indeed, every canny shopper knows that September is the best time to pick up bargain previously owned electrical goods from their local Crack Converters.

Now, far be it from me to suggest that you should just wait in your hallway with an airgun all through the summer months in case someone slips their fingers though the letterbox, just out of householder paranoia, but it's really just the same as birdwatching in Scotland or something, except there's less chance of rain. As long as you have a hot flask of Bovril on the landing during those chilly early mornings, it really is an option to be considered.

---

* All that 'slipping a credit card into the Yale lock' pantomime is considered rather old hat these days.

5 foreign coins that will end up in a jar in your bedroom

There's little doubt that, at some point in the not-too distant future, we'll all have our financial worth burned into
a chip implanted somewhere on our bodies. It will make
it much harder to lose your purse, and muggers won't have
to scuff up their fists on our faces. They'll probably just
empty our wallets wirelessly and the world will be a
better place. Until then, though, we'll still have to con-
tend with dirty cash. And, more to the point, dirty foreign
cash. Bureaux de change are very happy to take a small
commission for exchanging our sterling notes for ones
that we can use wherever we're going, and they're equally
happy to take another commission for exchanging the foreign notes we've miraculously managed not to use when
we come back.

What they don't want, though, is change. No one
does, really. It's ghastly greasy stuff, all covered in other
people's sebum and pocket fluff. So you end up bringing a
surprising tonnage of useless currency home. It wouldn't
be so bad if foreign money was distinctive, so that, when
you're fumbling for some cash at Heathrow tube, you
don't end up trying to put what is effectively, at this stage,
a load of scrap metal into the ticket machines while other
stressed-out ex-holidaymakers tut and sigh behind you.
Distinctive, though, is just what it isn't.

Exhibit A The US quarter. Similar enough to the current UK 10p to pass a cursory visual examination, but lacking the weight or authority to deceive our splendid London Underground ticketing machines. Of course, you'll never think to pay for anything with a quarter while you're in America, preferring instead to pull out a fat sheaf of essentially indistinguishable notes every time you buy anything, routinely handing over $100s, which you think are one dollar bills. The quarters, meanwhile, will mount up in your pocket, dangerously affecting the balance of the aircraft on the return journey.

Exhibit B The European 5 cent piece. Looks like a penny, and feels like a penny. Is even of similarly negligible value to a penny. When you're trying to catch up on two weeks' news, though, try handing a few of these to the man at the paper stall for a refreshing reminder of some choice English expressions you haven't heard in a while.

Exhibit C The US 1 cent piece. Effectively valueless at its point of origin, even more valueless, annoying and encrusted with a mysterious verdigris 3,000 miles from home.

Exhibit D The Hong Kong dollar. Feels enough like a 2p when you've just got off a thirteen-hour flight. Enough to mark you out as some sort of evil confidence trickster when it's mixed in with the handful of change you offer, in all innocence, to the *Big Issue* guy at the tube on your first day back at work. You're going to have to walk past him twice a day for the rest of your life. Now *that*'s something to look forward to.

Exhibit E The euro. Doesn't look, taste or feel like anything. Is theoretically worth about 60p in your local Marks and Spencers. Just try it, go on. See where it gets you.

THINGS YOU CAN ONLY DO @ HOME #12:
How to cope without your PlayStation

The compulsion to shed one's quotidian responsibilities and escape to a place where normal rules do not apply is well-nigh irresistible to some people. Which is why millions of people the world over (well, the bit of the world with enough infrastructure and disposable income to be eligible) buy themselves a games console or a nice computer and disappear for hours at a time into entirely imaginary worlds. These worlds aren't (yet) completely immersive, but they offer sufficient suspension of disbelief that you can often see see *Halo* players twitching in their seats as they dodge phantom bullets or *Gran Turismo* addicts leaning into imaginary curves as they race around a track that exists only inside their PlayStation*.

It's not uncommon for the better halves of the men (and it nearly is always men) that are tempted in this direction to disapprove of this pastime. This would be a mistake. The good thing about a video game addict is that at least the wives of these electronically delinquent husbands know where they *are* of an evening, and although a modern games console will generally cost a couple of hundred pounds, they more than pay for themselves over the course of their six-month lifespan in nights not had down the pub and horses not wagered upon. Plus, they have been 'proven' by 'experts' to sharpen up reaction time and contribute to much later bed-times, which means that the woman of the house is rarely troubled for anything untoward in the nightie area.

Alas, all this is lost once the home is forsaken for some holiday chalet. The video game addict will start to feel withdrawal symptoms on or around the third day. These can take the form of visual disturbances, where a phantom health and ammo counter appear in the peripheral vision, or just plain twitchiness and boredom. Displacement activities, like the consumption of excessive amounts of treacherous lager and unwanted disarraying of the nightie are the inevitable consequences of this deprivation.

---

* A little bit like the idealised images you see in holiday brochures, which depict hotels that only exist in the wildly optimistic dreams of travel agents.

If you really want to avoid all this unpleasantness, there are really only two choices. Buy a mobile games device – the PSP is about the prettiest of the bunch, I would suggest – or select a break with all of the amenities of home. Like at home, for example.

7 films that dare to tell the truth about holidays

Midnight Express The classic 'tourist in trouble' tale. Based on the true story of Billy Hayes, an American backpacker who fell foul of Turkish Customs and ended up being sentenced to thirty years in an astoundingly nasty prison. The lessons we can learn from this film, if any, are (1) you should never attempt to smuggle drugs, or even go over your Duty Free allowance if travelling via Turkey, and (2) rubbing your boobs on a plate glass window can be terribly romantic if you do it right.

Deliverance The Chatooga River stands in for the film's imaginary Cahulawassee River but, in every other respect, the film is effectively true. It tells the story of four suburban men on one of those special manly holidays that Americans favour, where everyone wears a vile check shirt and shoots at animals. They have a run in with some authentically inbred yokels who are good at the banjo and even better, it transpires, at sodomy and are so keen to demonstrate their prowess that they cannot wait politely for an invitation, as (for example) an Englishman might. Mayhem ensues. People get shot. No postcards are sent. All in all, a predictably unsatisfying adventure holiday.

The Wicker Man More yokels, this time Scottish ones. Edward Woodward plays an ordinary copper who (unwisely, in my view) has never taken the time to read *The Golden Bough* and, as a consequence, ends up in a vast and terrible basketwork barbecue affair. The lesson here is, study J. G. Frazer and study him well. Knowledge of ancient European or Aztec folk rituals may one day save your life.

Southern Comfort Men who are old enough to know better play war games in the woods and fall foul of yet *more* yokels. There's a message here, and frankly every Millets customer needs to think long and hard about what that message might be.

Thelma and Louise Cross-country road trip ends in tragedy. It's funny because it's true.

Planes, Trains and Automobiles A film that takes the basic 'Out of Towners' template of mounting travel frustration and adds the horror of getting saddled with a corpulent bore who thinks he's your friend. You can be sure that this film, along with *Flight 93*, *Alive*, *No Highway in the Sky*, *Airport 1975*, *Flight of the Phoenix*, *Airplane 2* or, indeed, *Pushing Tin* will never be selected as your in-flight movie.

Frantic If you've ever lost a laptop, family member, some traveller's cheques or your favourite sunglasses on holiday, this film tells your story.

Excess baggage #2: How you'll end up bringing all of that foreign food home

I regret to inform you, dear reader, that you have found the toilet humour section. It was bound* to happen eventually. Whether you've bought yourself a paperback spinoff from some Radio 4 panel show where brainy people remind you which memorable sayings come from Shakespeare and which ones were made up by Groucho Marx (it's always one of the two) or you find yourself inadvertently reading one of those witless, classless and mercifully authorless 'parodies' of a popular bestseller which are aimed exclusively at the myopic gift-buyer in a hurry, there's always a point where the writer runs a bit low on

---

* Bound! He said bound!

ideas and pads the manuscript out with some stuff about bums. *A Midsummer Night's Dream* is full of it, for example. And so, regrettably, is this book. Here it comes.

If you drink a little more alcohol than usual while you're away (and frankly, who doesn't?), you'll become a trifle dehydrated. This can lead to constipation, which is never glamorous. If you tend to eat richer food on holiday than you might at home (and if you don't, then why do you bother going?), your digestion will tend to slow down. This can lead to trapped wind, which is hardly *chic*. If you are one of those sensitive flowers who prefer to perform their most intimate acts on their own facilities, a certain amount of performance anxiety may also well ensue when faced with exotic plumbing fixtures.

The net result is that, by the end of the first week of your holiday, you will be visiting popular tourist attractions with a painfully distended stomach and trailing a malodorous miasma of your own making. If you imagined for even a moment that romance might blossom anew between you and your partner while on holiday, then you clearly imagined a holiday where she wasn't up every night rinsing out the only trousers she has that have an elasticated waistband and praying to get home as soon as possible so she can have the house to herself and settle down for a genuinely epic poo. After all, hotel rooms are notoriously intimately configured, and nobody likes an audience.

How people who live in hotels all the time manage with their toilet arrangements is beyond the remit of this volume, but all the best reading room visits happen in one's own home. If you've just got home from holiday, you'd better take another book. This one probably won't be long enough. Not unless I put a few more fart gags in.

THINGS YOU CAN ONLY DO @ HOME #13:
Be gay

Because what you do once you've had your cocoa and said your prayers is a deeply personal matter, there are no absolutely accurate figures on how many gay people there are in the UK. Not everyone who is gay thinks of it as a full-time job either, so, even if you asked them, they might have a more complicated answer than you could fit on a form. The best guesses average around 5 per cent of the population, so, in the UK, we're probably looking at somewhere in the region of three million or so people. These three million people have more or less as much holiday time as the rest of us. Slightly less, admittedly, because, as I understand it, being gay involves quite a few really brilliant nights out, so chances are the homosexual community are obliged to set aside a couple more days than us ordinary people just to have a bit of a lie-in occasionally, and that rather eats into the standard annual entitlement.

In the UK, for quite some time now, we have treated our homosexualists more or less as equals – generally poor at jobs like demolition and bus driving and so forth, but, then again, frequently terrific at pop music, comedy and having new ideas for frocks, so it all evens out. We British are, as a general rule, (quite sensibly) proud of our gay people and they, in turn, are, broadly speaking, rather proud of being British. Overseas, though, attitudes vary. Two men holding hands in Soho won't even get a second look. They might elicit a raised eyebrow in Huddersfield, perhaps, but the same simple act of companionship in many popular holiday destinations will probably precipitate the formation of an angry mob with flaming torches and catchy chants. Two people of the same gender booking a room with a double bed will be met with varying levels of resistance according to the distance of said bed from north London, in accordance with (as previously discussed) Moran's Law.

Honestly, if gayness is your thing, you're best off picking a nice city break where you can be assured of a little more understanding. Perhaps you could choose a city where people speak your language too, which helps if you're asking for advice about where you can go for a really brilliant night out. Now, where are there lots of cities where people speak English? If your answer was 'America', you need to think again. *Will and Grace* wasn't a documentary.

Vacation roulette: The group holiday

When you're in your 20s, or even in your 30s, it seems like the most obvious idea in the world: get together a bunch of those people who seem like such fun when you meet them in the pub and take them all away on holiday *so you can go to the pub every night*! No boring work to get up in the morning for! It'll be like one long episode of *Friends*, except with more liver damage. People will be popping out witticisms every minute on the minute and everyone will get on like a blazing hostel. Right?

Wrong. The thing about being in your 20s, or even (I find) your 40s, is that you're essentially the same solipsistic and emotionally volatile idiot you were in your teens, except with more commitments to distract you from periodic outbreaks of sulky rage and a lot more disposable income to blow on intoxicants that will bring out the worst in you. Remove the restraint of work from the equation and you can be sure that, even if you personally aren't in a mood with one or other of your travelling companions, two of them definitely will have fallen out about some issue at once unfathomable and trivial. Worse, mixed-sex groups will inevitably include at least one couple who will treat the break as the ideal opportunity to publicly re-enact the entirety of either

Nine Songs or *Who's Afraid of Virginia Woolf*, neither of which make for inclusive entertainment.

Even worse than all that, though, is the single-sex group: female travellers may all have been footloose and fancy free back in May when the tickets were cheap but, by July, at least one of the company will want to spend every spare minute moping silently for the wannabe DJ called Drew they met the week before they flew out or else obsessively texting throughout every meal and rather putting a dampener on the proceedings. Their male counterparts will find it somewhat easier to forget about the PR assistant to whom they recently declared undying love in All Bar One, but instead will have every meal ruined by peer-pressure from the one loser who still lives with his mum and overcompensates by suggesting tequila slammer contests and trips to the local brothel over breakfast and goes steadily downhill throughout the day.

Hell isn't other people. It's other people *on holiday*.

The unbearable shiteness of Center Parcs

Have you *seen* all those rough-hewn handrails that have been hacked from Amazonian rainforests just to make

C2-class consumers feel like they're closer to The Eden Project than Butlins? Splinter Parcs would be a better name for the place. Take any kid there on holiday and they'll come home with more foreign objects lodged under their skin than Kevin bloody Warwick.

3 habits of highly effective smugglers

Security in our air and sea ports is tighter than it's ever been. Before the World War I, you could go just about anywhere you fancied without a passport or much interference from Her Majesty's Customs. Now you have to book an extra day at either end of your holiday just so the Government can be sure you're not a shoe bomber. Not that any of this inconvenience achieves anything. Have you ever met a drug dealer that was out of stock? For that matter, the grey economy that drives the catering and domestic service industries is reliant on smuggled people that are all a good deal bulkier than a block of Semtex or a wrap of Keith Richards' granddad. I know I've been fairly dismissive of the whole travel caper up to now, but just to show I can be constructive if I want to, here's how smugglers get all that stuff we're not supposed to have across our borders. They just follow these three simple rules:

1 Don't use cosmetics . . .

Every British airport has one these days: a vast Perspex monolith full of plastic bottles with the proud legend – 'Over one million items seized!' Brilliant. No one's yet brought down an airliner with Head and Shoulders, and there's no thriving overseas black market for Timotei that I'm aware of. So what's it for? Was it put there by a superior civilisation to push us to the next evolutionary level? Or by security goons who want to impress you with how incredibly efficient they are at confiscating evening primrose oil? Frankly, if the women of Britain can't take casefuls of cosmetics so they can make themselves up as Bratz dolls while they're on their holidays, then the terrorists have already won. They really have. If Western women aren't in a position to use a little dab of Touche Éclat after a hard night on the rosé, they're going to be that little bit more amenable to the idea of wearing a veil to cover the odd blemish. Next stop Sharia law. I digress. All I'm saying is, if you want a swift passage through airport security, don't bring conditioner.

2 . . . but do use plenty of deodorant

The 'nothing to declare' chicane may seem like a quiet and strangely pointless stage on your way out of the airport, but there's a lot more going on than you imagine: the shadowy figures behind the mirrored windows aren't just mooning the oblivious passengers. Oh no. They're watching for perspiration. When Kennedy and Nixon staged the first televised presidential debate in 1960, voters all over America saw the sweat break out on Nixon's lip and they knew, instantly, he was the wrong sort. And they only had to wait until 1973 to be proved right. A sweaty lip is a sure sign of guilt. Just look at that Barry White. The poor chap was probably body-searched more times than you've had disappointing tapas. So, if you don't want your bag searched, empty a can of Right Guard into your face before you check your bags. Then throw the can away (see rule 1).

3 Find a compliant mule

'Did you pack these bags yourself, sir?' What a silly question. No man packs his own bags. If he's married, his wife does it, because he can't be trusted. If he's single, his magical alter ego (the one that comes out when he's had a couple of Stellas) does it in those few frantic minutes between realising that he's going on holiday tomorrow and passing out. If he's any kind of man at all, his valet will have done it. You can plant anything in a man's suitcase, because he won't really look in it anyway. Wearing the same pair of pants for a week is one of the perks of being on holiday, and any T-shirt worthy of the name can go at least a few wears, unless someone's sick on it. Women, being the more romantic sex, are easier to seduce into carrying a half-hundredweight of Afghan crack back to Preston, but, unfortunately, being the better groomed sex, are more likely to be searched by cynical customs officers looking for a nice bit of nearly-new Clarins for the wife (see rule 1).

Remember, though, if you do get caught trying to import something you're not supposed to, you've never heard of me. And if you don't get caught, can you get me some? Chad and Bradley were out of stock again.

Come on, we don't even speak *English* properly yet!

The last week or so before a foreign holiday is typified by frantic mugging up on the phrasebook, as if a handful of strangely irrelevant phrases about trams will suddenly confer upon the reader the cosmopolitan air of a seasoned jetsetter. Why do we do it to ourselves? According to a poll commissioned for the BBC last year, only 2 per cent of Britons can ask how to find the toilet in the main language they learned at school (French generally, although a few Quisling colleges still put a fair bit of effort into German). More critical than where you're going seems to be where you're from: Midlanders are quite game apparently, but while about 40 per cent of Londoners know the word for 'beer' in more than one foreign language, regrettably only 3 per cent of them would then be able to express an apology in that same language should events take a turn for the lively. The majority of Scots, however, avoid speaking any foreign languages at all. The survey isn't clear on whether they're including English in that.

In my entirely unscientific tests, as a result of the curious nature of the human brain, any attempt to learn a foreign language in a hurry only bears fruit about a month after the holiday is over, so you will suddenly find yourself saying ¡gracias! by accident to a confused-looking bus driver in Stratford Road, B28, leading to a significant majority of the other bus patrons concluding that you're a rather pretentious cove, and certainly not the type of person to be trusted.

Meanwhile, linguists believe that, of the 6,000 or so languages spoken today, at least half will be extinct by 2100. With the increased penetration of English as a result of the exponential expansion of the Internet, we can be fairly sure that it will only take about half that time again to see off the remaining few thousand.

Now. If we look after ourselves, keep away from stressful situations, like airport check-ins, railway termini and language classes, we could probably live another hundred years with the way medicine is advancing.

So all you have to do is hang on, not much more than a hundred years or so, and you can travel anywhere you like without learning so much as a word in any other language at all. That'll leave plenty of brain room free to learn how to drive your personal hovercraft and remember which colour pill is the Sunday lunch. Result.

Purgatory on wheels: The long drive

The term 'family saloon' is a curious one. Certainly there's ample room for an average family in one, if they're just puttering off to the garden centre or something, that is – it's only when you try to fit in sufficient changes of clothes for two weeks, some toys to keep the youngest amused and (God forbid) a tent that it becomes a cramped and sweltering torture chamber that improves upon the traditional Thai prison 'hot box' only by being mobile and packed with people who are trying to give you a dead leg without Mum noticing. Everybody in the vehicle will be trying to distract themselves with radios, mints and fun activities: these generally take the form of Dad (traditionally) driving, Mum (as is the custom) in the shotgun seat wrestling with a map the size of a picnic blanket and two point four kids busy pinching each other in the back seat and trying to avoid the impartial fury of the Disembodied Parental Hand that flails periodically between the seatbacks and smites guilty and innocent alike.

Another key aspect of the holiday car journey is that it's so much longer than any normal voyage you might normally undertake, thereby exposing any shortcomings in the vehicle's upholstery. You will find that, should you have any small children in the car, a correctly-fitted booster seat is particularly uncomfortable for the final thirty-six hours or so of a drive to Cornwall (which, in defiance of geography, geometry, and, for all I know, geology, is further away from everywhere on earth than the fucking moon), which will lead to an incessant piteous whimpering from the occupant that no standard car stereo – no matter how splendidly appointed – can drown out. You might think that the ideal sonic accompaniment to a long-distance car journey would be the steady thwack of ever-larger and more alien-looking insects dying in the attempt to smash through your windscreen punctuated by the rarer, more apocalyptic slam of the occasional paving stone dropped from an overpass by a bored yokel. You would be mistaken. The most suitable soundtrack to any lengthy motor voyage is whatever's on Radio 2 at the time, cranked up to within a few decibels of the average human's pain threshold. You wonder why the commoner sort of person puts speakers the size of wardrobes* in their cars? It's not just to be anti-social,

* The cavernous speaker cabinets also double as a handy receptacle when the inevitable travel sickness kicks in just as the car is equidistant between two sets of services. Middle-class ponces like you and me have to make do with a hastily emptied panini wrapper, which will, of course, have a hole in it somewhere to prevent small children suffocating. The manufacturers clearly don't realise that, at the moment when the whey-faced child announces that they're going to throw up, there's nothing the parents would like more than to humanely asphyxiate their offspring.

it's because they know that, sooner or later, they're going to be transporting a toddler for a considerable distance (to Askham Grange to visit their mum, perhaps) and (to their credit) they're planning ahead. Bravo! Johnny Council, with your life-threateningly loud in-car entertainment!

As our budget airlines become increasingly oversubscribed, even the more modest trip to the airport becomes a feat of endurance and fortitude worthy of the great Renaissance explorers. Both of the biggest airports in Britain are placed within a few miles of our most poorly thought-out motorway, guaranteeing interminable traffic jam tedium which the passing of no quantity of transitorily thrilling Eddie Stobart lorries can alleviate. You might just make it to the airport in time to be told that your flight is overbooked, but you're just as likely to spend the first few hours of your holiday wandering along the hard shoulder asking drivers of suspicious-looking Range Rovers if they've got a pistol in their glove compartment so you can end it all.

Modern cars are supposedly designed to be as comfortable and filled with entertainment options as your living room, except on wheels. The thing is, if the wheels are going to remain essentially stationary for much of the time, you can pretty much forget them – at which point your living room is likely to be the more luxurious and cost-effective option.

Sod abroad: Holidays in space

Let's not dwell too much on the absolutely unconscionable pricing structure of current space tourism offerings. It's a good deal more than you and I earn in a year put together, I'll tell you that much. Then again, the first air passenger flew less than a hundred years ago, and airlines didn't really get going until the 1920s. Now, less than eighty years later, we have easyJet and Monarch flying the commoner sort of person all over the world. Space tourism is still an expensive proposition now, but that will change sooner than you think. By the time you're a pensioner (which at the current rate of advance, will be in your late 90s), the kids vandalising your fusion-powered shopmobility scooter will all be wearing silver overalls bearing the words: 'The technician who squirted a pipette of nutrients into my Petri dish went to the moon and all I got was this lousy spacesuit'.

In the short term, though, it's only a viable prospect for slightly nerdy billionaires. If you, by some odd chance, *are* some sort of slightly nerdy billionaire who is thinking about having himself briefly catapulted into low orbit, why not buy *another* copy of this fine book and I'll explain to you why not to bother, and, as a bonus, give you a top-notch suggestion for a far better way to squander your wealth.

First of all, the other, less frequently mentioned, expense of modern space flight is its really quite significant ecological cost. Conservative estimates put the emissions from a short suborbital flight at around three tonnes per passenger. That's something like the carbon footprint of a flight from, say, London to Singapore. If you switched off every electric device in your lovely mansion for four or five years, you could easily make that up. Remember, though that you're unlikely to be taking off from the UK, because our dreams of manned space flight were effectively cancelled a few weeks before the first Dan Dare comic was printed (1950, fact fans!). Consequently, you'll probably have to add on the CO_2 load of a flight to the US or (if you really have no fear) Russia as well. That's about another two and a half years of no electricity before you're carbon neutral on this trip. Best not take a digital camera into space then, because there'll be no way of powering the interminably dull laptop slideshow when you get home and the millionaires next door come round for some mulled wine and a look at your holiday snaps.

Also, there's the question of being prepared. We subconsciously select holiday destinations based on our previous experience of similar locations: we know that New York will be a bit like London, only with better-dressed criminals; Miami is essentially a warm Manchester; Madrid is Brighton with tapas. But what's space like? Is it *really* like nothing you've ever experienced before? Well, not exactly. Space is like when your big sister tried to shut you in the fridge, only without gravity. Or any nice food. But *with* a moderate chance of being incinerated on re-entry.

Basically, if you've got in the region of twenty million quid to burn and you're looking for a bit of a thrill that you can show off about, just buy a bankrupt funfair and a job lot of chicken wire. Connect the chicken wire to the National Grid, stretch the wire about ten feet off the ground all across your nearest major city, and lend all your mates a dodgem each. You'll have the best laugh imaginable and people will be talking about how unbelievably cool you are for years to come. Which is all you really wanted, isn't it?

Travel broadens the mind

You probably had this idea that when you went abroad you'd meet interesting people from other cultures and learn from them. As if. See those people in the queue for check in? The ones with the really annoying hyperactive kid? You're spending the next two weeks with *them*.

THINGS THAT DO NOT MIX #1: Sex and the beach

No matter what purveyors of single-entendre-based cocktails might have you believe, sex on the beach is not all it's cracked up to be. Although your presence on the beach generally presupposes a degree of *déshabillé*, which makes the prospect of coition both more enticing and apparently achievable, there are a number of obstacles to successful congress. Assuming that you have embarked on such an enterprise spontaneously, you will first have a privacy problem to negotiate. This is not insurmountable, with a careful choice of timing (after dark is best) and location (between a couple of good-sized sand dunes). The addition of a convenient freestanding windbreak is also a plus. Once you have all these things, though, although the beach as a whole cannot see you, you will not be able to see much of the beach – effectively rendering the 'on the beach' element of the endeavour somewhat null and void. Also, despite its much-vaunted sterility, the sandy environment of the beach plays host to a distressingly large population of annoyingly hoppy and jumpy insects who will all be keen to gatecrash the intimate occasion. Ignoring the possible necessity for acquiring a condom in the vicinity, should one be required, you will still have a clothing storage issue to overcome and then, of course, ultimately, the unamusing presence of gritty sand in intimate folds which are not specified to deal with grit of any nature. There will probably be sand in your socks too, assuming you took them off, and I sincerely hope you did. All in all, sex on the beach is a better drink than an activity, and it's a pretty terrible drink.

The lie that speaks the truth: *EastEnders* on holiday

It is a universally accepted truth that *EastEnders* is the most appalling piffle. If we are to watch it, we are required to believe that there is an improbably monocultural small enclave of people living in the Bromley-by-Bow area. As you have probably observed yourself when inadvertently watching an episode, these people live in quite desirable properties that have mysteriously avoided the great wave of gentrification that engulfed the area in the 1980s and 1990s. Despite living in such premium real estate, they don't, in the main, own washing machines. Most of the denizens of Walford also live and work in the same post-code, and they buy the substantial part of their weekly shop in a small corner store that has retained independence in a commercial climate that has seen virtually every retail space in the Greater London area turned into a Tesco Metro, or a Starbucks, or both. Many of the inhabitants of Albert Square even dress exclusively in items purchased from a market stall that are, uniquely among market stall items, not emblazoned with misspelled designer logos. None of them, even more surprisingly, support Premier League football teams or have a favourite television programme either. But, most improbably of all, these supposed Londoners actually *talk* to one another. It's a simplification to suggest that they live in a time warp. The London depicted in *Eastenders* has never existed except in the imagination of a fluid group of scriptwriters who keep forgetting which characters are which* or where they're supposed to be from.

But, there is one aspect of *Eastenders* which teaches us something of value. For the inhabitants of Walford, holidays always end in misery: Den and Angie in Venice, 1986 – the tipping point when their dysfunctional marriage finally collapsed into infidelity, alcoholism and medical deceit; the Beales in Devon, 1990 – comedy shotgun cottage showdown; the Mitchells in Paris, 1993 – more marital mishaps; the Fowlers in Amsterdam, 1993 – drug smuggling ineptitude; assorted characters in Torremolinos, 1995 – predictable Iberian pratfalls. The list goes on practically ad infinitum. These lovable cockneys can barely leave their postcode without falling off a cliff or being involved in a terrible car accident, it seems.

The thing is, whereas every other aspect of the show is a lazily scripted Punch-and-Judy show for the indolent poor, when it comes to coverage of holidays, it's practically a documentary. The writers evidently feel that whereas, in the main, their output is so comically unrealistic as to make *Star Trek* look like a Ken Loach film,

---

* And, indeed, what they've done. Phil Mitchell drove the getaway car for a bank robbery a few years back, a new shift of writers clocked on and the old ones went home without leaving a note about it – it's never been mentioned since.

there is one truth so unavoidable that to ignore it would stretch the credulity of their audience beyond breaking point. It is this: leave the city and it will end in tears. If you learn nothing else from our fine Public Service Broadcasting system, learn this.

Sex tourists: How to spot one, and how not to get mired in a 4-hour conversation with one

There are some perfectly good reasons to visit Thailand, Ghana or the Caribbean. I just can't imagine what they might be. Perhaps you might have an enthusiasm for freakishly large insects, or exotic and effectively untreatable diseases? Thailand, certainly, is a popular stopover for aeroplanes exhausted by the effort of flying all the way to the Antipodes, which are, as we will see, further from anywhere you care to name than any other holiday destination. Except Cornwall, obviously.

Unfortunately, a significant number of people who visit these 'pleasure spots' are – to be as kind as I can about it – desperately inadequate losers who think it's OK to exploit people of poorer economies in the interest of a quick shag. You're not one of those sad types, obviously, but if you find yourself in one of these locations – or

Tijuana for Americans and (implausibly) Vladivostok for our Japanese cousins – then there's every chance you're going to accidentally meet one of them.

Now, they've demonstrated an inability to cop off with the likes of you and me by the very act of buying their ticket and, as we non-losers know the key to copping off is having the ability to maintain an interesting conversation – well, that and having really nice shoes, obviously – consequently getting trapped in a conversation with one of these oily oddballs is a fate most assiduously to be avoided.

The easiest way to spot one is if they're carrying a book called *Travel and the Single Male* by an undoubtedly splendid gentleman called Bruce Cassier. It isn't easy to come by, so, if you see someone with it, they haven't just picked it up in WH Smiths at the airport by chance. As yet there's no shadowy organisation of Gary Glitter Gideons leaving copies in hotel rooms either, so it's a sure bet that ownership of this volume more or less confirms the holder as some sort of peripatetic pervert. For the more pretentious end of the market, there's an equally strong showing for Michel Houellebecq's *Platform*, which has all the detachment, amorality and outright fruitiness one might expect from Johnny Frenchman, and has a young miss in tight pants on the cover in case you're too dizzily priapic to read the blurb. There's no equivalent guidebook for female sex tourists, however, although they are increasing in number more rapidly than their male counterparts. Perhaps, given the crypto-racist subtext of their proclivities, you might catch one with a paperback about ante-bellum Southern plantations: one of the Falconhurst books perhaps, or *Gone with the bloody Wind*. Or you could just ask them if you can get Klan outfits in a size 14.

Essentially, these people are Nazis, and not even Nazis like to hang around with Nazis. They'll try to dress it up with pretendy egalitarian conversational gambits*, but at heart they're goose-stepping fascists in sunhats. The imagined separation between people with different tints of tan enables them to think of the people they're exploiting as commodities, which of course makes it all OK. The sex tourist also tends to be travelling on his or her own, will have been to the resort before and so will know all the best places to go and (if applicable) a few key phrases in the local lingo, and (if male) will have a Hawaiian shirt – all of which (except the shirt) makes them a useful person to bump into on the first day of your holiday, but, by day four, you will have heard about their messy divorce several dozen times and you'll have no chance of shaking

---

* Here's a stock quote to watch for: 'It's funny, but in England, the girls I fancy don't fancy me and the ones that do fancy me, I don't fancy. They tend to be sort of fatter and older, you know, thirty-five, but their faces, they look forty. But, in Cuba, really beautiful girls fancy me. They're all over me. They treat me like a star.' What they're really saying is: 'Candidly, I'm a bit of a beast, and the only people that I can attract back home are fairly rough too – but while my £35k a year IT job makes me look a pretty poor catch in Guildford, I'm effectively a golden god in a backwater like this.'

them off, short of deliberately getting bitten by a barracuda and being evacuated back home by your travel insurance providers (which is the holiday equivalent of chewing your arm off to get out of a bear trap, unless you are on holiday in Canada, in which case chewing your arm off to get out of a bear trap is the equivalent of chewing your arm off to get out of a bear trap). A barracuda can give you a pretty nasty nip, but all things being taken into consideration, it's probably worth it.

Wherever you're going, your suitcase is going somewhere better

As steeply as the curve rises on graphs plotting the increase of air passenger numbers, the line showing how many pieces of luggage are going astray is rising even more sharply*. According to a crude graph I've just scribbled on a Caffè Nero napkin, at some point in the middle of this century, the two lines will cross and every single person who travels by air will lose his or her luggage. Soon after that, in a development that defies understanding,

---

* Recent figures from the Air Transport Users Council show passengers lose (or, more correctly, have lost for them) approximately thirty million bags a year, and it's getting steadily worse.

more bags will get lost than are actually dispatched. That seems silly, I know, but that's not *me* saying that – that's *maths* talking, and maths doesn't lie.

So what are we going to do about it? Well, we've got a couple of choices, actually. First, we can build a GPS and a mobile phone into every suitcase so that the case can call the owner and tell them which unclaimed luggage auction it's in and how much extra profit it's going to make for the airline that lost it. That's liable to be a bit pricey, at least at first, and may well fall foul of airline security regulations against having complicated telecommunications devices in the hold that could (a) just as easily be used to detonate a bomb as they could to locate a set of golf clubs and (b) adversely affect the revenue from lost luggage auctions. The second choice, and you're probably ahead of me on this one by now, is just not to bother. After all, apart from the odd sock in the washing machine, you don't tend to lose so many clothes at home.

It's all computers now, isn't it? The treacheries of technology

'*Oh brave new world, that hath such boss stuff in 't.*' That's what Shakespeare said, more or less, and he'd never even *seen* a Currys. The proliferation of computers and tiny devices that might as well be computers means that we can communicate with one another as a species more easily than at any time since our ancestors wandered out of Ethiopia on a fishing trip some 90,000 years ago, forgot the way home and, after several rather heated discussions about who was in charge of the map and whether anyone had remembered to bring any sandwiches, decided to spread across the globe. The opportunities to share ideas and culture using the Internet are unprecedented in history.

So what do we do with it? Well, most Internet traffic consists of people offering to sell you Viagra (or at least Viagra-like substances that may or may not give you a heart attack) and, of course, international banking. Now, if you thought that we might be talking about Viagra in this bit, you've picked up the wrong book. Those short-lived erections on the cover are sandcastles. International money transfer is the issue here. Does it work? Yes. Does it work for you? Listen carefully, and the distant laughter of well-fed bankers drifting on the wind from the Square Mile will answer your question.

If you decide to be all modern and use your credit card overseas rather than carry around bales of the Early Learning Centre money that the Bureau de Change man *assures* us that people use in Martinique, you might expect to pay the going exchange rate for the money you use, perhaps with a small commission to keep the poor International Banking community in stripy shirts.

You might prefer to continue believing that, rather than delving into the Byzantine complexities of foreign loading fees and dynamic currency conversion. Obviously, this is a subject that you should be consulting a grown-up about, rather than relying on a lightweight like me, but the gist of it is this: you go out for a delicious meal somewhere like . . . say . . . Rome and are presented with a bill for about . . . say . . . eighty euros. You've already had a couple of grappas by this time, so your imperfect maths gets as far as telling you that it comes to about fifty quid before you dismiss it with an airy (metaphorical) wave and hand the waiting waiter your Visa card and he pops it into that funny wireless thing while you carry on talking to your companion about something interesting. Not about exchange rates, that's for certain. You've already forgotten about them. Doubly so when, after your payment is processed, there can be no more charge levied upon your card when the restaurateur sends another couple of complimentary grappas your way. 'What a thoroughly decent chap,' you think, as you sip the fiery spirit and weave back to your hotel, at which point you forget about even that and start thinking about how you probably should have replied to one of those emails offering you some Viagra because all those grappas seem to have had a deleterious effect on the old gentleman's gentleman this evening. You certainly won't remember the exact details of the evening when your credit card statement drops through the letterbox about a month or so later, but certainly the figure in pounds sterling seems a lot higher than you imagined when you (miraculously) managed to type your PIN in correctly all those weeks ago. That's because the restaurateur had applied a *soupçon* of dynamic currency conversion when he processed your payment and basically charged you an exchange rate that he'd made up with his admirable Italian imagination. It could be worse, through, you could have noticed something untoward at the time and telephoned your bank about it. Then your mobile phone operator would have taken a sizeable bite out of you as well.

Still, at least you can save a bit of money by booking online, eh? Well. Possibly. That can quite easily work against you too. There was a *Sunday Times* journalist called Bob Tyrer who tried that. You'd be surprised how close the F and R keys are together on the keyboard. A small typographical error, in which he misspelt his name as 'Tyrfer', nearly ended up costing him £2,270 for replacement tickets. Luckily for him, the airline caved in after several dozen increasingly scary telephone calls that mentioned his place of employment and the dire consequences of crossing a person who works at one of the most trusted news sources on earth. The thing is, you know your name pretty well, so you tend to assume you've typed it properly. It could happen to anyone. If that 'anyone' is you, and you don't have the mighty weight of our great nation's newspaper of record behind you, best double check before you press 'OK'.

The Internet's rubbish, isn't it? I'd get rid of it, if I didn't need the Viagra.

THINGS YOU CAN ONLY DO @ HOME #14: E-commerce

Have I mentioned how absolutely marvellous the Internet is? Not only can you read reviews of hotels and restaurants that have been covertly written by hoteliers and restaurateurs, but you can also buy all sorts of stuff. Ridiculous gadgets of doubtful utility, T-shirts that no one else you know has, amusing mock-travel books that didn't quite make the bestseller lists, all sorts. It's just wonderful. The only thing is, once you've entered your credit card details into that website that keeps reassuring you how secure it is, your retail fate is in the hands of a rather slipshod organisation called the Royal Mail. Assuming whatever you've decided to buy wasn't considered interesting enough to be stolen at the sorting office (statistical analysis says that this book falls into that category), there will be one somewhat desultory attempt to deliver the item to your address, or an address that was in some way similar to yours. Woe betide you web-savvy purchasers that were out at work when the postman called, because, once he has followed the magical trail of red rubber bands back to his lair, you will be drawn into a Kafkaesque spiral of repeat delivery requests and attempts to visit a wildly oversubscribed parcel collection facility that is open only for two minutes every alternate Tuesday.

There's only one way to make the Internet work for you: take a couple of weeks off. Embark on an online spending spree safe in the knowledge that you won't be going on holiday this year so you'll have plenty of disposable income and lie in wait behind your front door for the postman. You'll soon have cooler gadgets than everyone you know and have something to read on the train when you eventually go back to work rested, free from skin cancer and wearing a really sweet T-shirt.

The loneliness of the long-distance shopper

Of course you cancelled the milk while you were away. It's only sensible. You'll be too tired to do a shop on that first evening back, though, which means, on that first morning, you'll have to walk the streets at the crack of dawn trying to find a shop that opens up early so you can have a nice cup of coffee. As you wander the quiet streets, with only birdsong and the distant tantalising hum of milk floats to distract you, you'll probably start thinking how lovely the old place is in that dayspring sun. It's only when the streets get crowded with people that your home town begins to lose its allure, and it's quite understandable that so many people want to live there, because it's so very nice, so overcrowding is just a symptom of success. You might come to thinking that, actually, where you live isn't so bad after all. Certainly a lot nicer than that infernal pit you've just come back from. And you'd be right.

When it all goes wrong, a board game will always make it worse

When everyone's got Freddy Krueger sunburn, when it's raining and you're stuck in your chalet, when you've twisted your ankle on the second day and you can't ski anymore, some idiot will always say the same thing:

'I know! Let's play a game.'

It's the same person that sacrificed valuable luggage space to the bulky box of eminently loseable plastic odds and ends which are an essential part of every modern board game. The problem is, only a precious few of us are well-adjusted enough to just chuck the dice down, accept the outcome with equanimity and sip modestly on a Heineken until it's our turn again. There are four distinct types of board game players that you'll encounter on holiday, therefore. Unless you count yourself, in which case there are five, but I'm assuming that you know what you're like. Here are the others:

1: The Barrack Room Lawyer The person who insists on reading every word of the rules printed on the inside of the box lid. Not just for quarter of an hour at the beginning of the game while everyone gets bored and tuts theatrically while rattling the dice for emphasis, but after each and every turn: otherwise how would you ever know that you're supposed to take a Star Value card, and then count the letters in the third word in the second paragraph on the card, then move back that many spaces unless you've got a Super Speedway card in which case you can move forward a distance equivalent to twice the amount of letters in the middle name of the person sitting to your left as long as the Golden Seismograph reads nine or above. Really. Life's too short.

2: The Spiv This is an individual for whom the rules are not so much a guide as an encumbrance. They will lie, cheat, trade Super Speedway cards with other players (see above) and generally subvert the rules of the game until it has no meaning at all. So why do they play? That's a question for the ages.

3: The Competitive Uncle A hybrid of the preceding two types. He will apply the rules assiduously when it comes to other players, but fudge shamelessly if it will advance his own cause. The easiest way to cope with the competitive uncle is to hand him the Golden Coaster at the beginning of the game and get on with reading whatever well-thumbed magazine you bought at the airport.

4: The Panglossian Mum She's the one who brought the game with her in the first place and she's the one that gets upset when people variously get pedantic about the rules, break the rules, get annoyingly competitive or disappear into the next room to drink Heinekens and read a magazine they've already read twice.

It's to The Panglossian Mum's credit that she anticipated the astonishingly dull experience you've all signed for, but the board game isn't the answer to the Great Holiday Problem. You know what is, don't you? Of course you do: you're holding it.

Venice is sinking: Under the weight of all that money

Even if you *can* afford the flight, and the transfers, and the hotel room, and the extortionately priced mineral water, I bet you'll still balk at handing over the compulsory extra payment for the buskers. Pizza Express will donate 25p on your behalf to save Venice from sinking? I'll pay McDonalds an extra quid if they'll promise to torpedo the place.

The holiday romance time bomb

Occupying a station in the moral spectrum roughly equidistant between the rapacious sex tourist and the slightly confused old lady who collects money for the cats' hospice, the premeditated vacation shagger is at the core of most holiday romances today. The modern busy professional has no time for Shirley Valentine's unplanned peregrinations from *taverna* to *taverna* until they are overpowered by either agapē or domestica (or, more commonly, both) and instead adopts a more goal-oriented approach. These are people who work hard, play hard, make contraception-related mistakes hard and by golly are willing to catch syphilis hard, if that's what it takes to have a good time.

This is all very well. If I am right (and I generally am) when I say holidays are one enormous mistake, then if one or two smaller mistakes are nested within them it matters little. The only problem occurs when the holidaymaking romancer makes the critical error of handing over a correct email or (worse) street address* as they begin their six-hundred-mile Walk Of Shame. This leaves the door open for a return visit from the romancee, which is scarcely equitable, because Person A (stay with me here) paid good money to stay in the country of Person B, but Person B will inevitably expect some sort of free ride when visiting Person A. These freeloading romancees have been known to turn up unexpectedly, looking distinctly less attractive when stripped of their attractive beach sunset backdrop, and expecting a cup of tea, or UK residency, or both.

Now, as a nation we have long prided ourselves on having attracted the brightest and most determined workers from across the globe to come and add their distinctiveness to our own. It's what's made this country the best there's ever been. If, however, we're going to start inviting people in on the basis of a well-turned ankle or the ability to say *signorina* in a winning way, then we run the risk of diluting our hard-working society with the cupidity of a bunch of attractive chancers. I know what you're going to say – if it's good enough for our dear Duke of Edinburgh then it's good enough for a slew of fruity-looking Russian brides, and I agree. The only work the Duke has ever done

* What they should be pressing into their inamorata's hand is the time-honoured brushoff phone number: 770 5519. The Continental method of forming the numeral '7' means that it works particularly well overseas. You'll be through customs before they think to look at it in a mirror.

is a spot of unlicensed minicabbing and, frankly, he's exactly the kind of person I'm against: keep letting in these work-shy royals and next thing you know our prized work ethic will be stuffed and there'll be a television show about people who are fairly easy on the eye but have nothing to offer intellectually and are looking to make a quick buck. Probably running all summer so that us determined stay-at-homers have to watch it. For all I know it'll be called something ridiculous like *Big Brother* or somesuch. That's exactly what caused the end of the Roman Empire and it'll do for us too, if we're not careful. All right, their overseas travel tended to take the form of campaigns of conquest rather than package tours, and their foreign imports were more frequently galley slaves who ended up fighting lions in the Colosseum rather than baristas who ended up having water fights on reality TV shows, but you see my point. The Romans tended to have lead in their drinking water rather than fluoride too, but I think the parallels are clear.

A man who is tired of London is probably right

Our great nation's capital has been my home since birth. It is a city with many virtues. Certainly there is a lengthy list of attractions which the tourist feels obliged to visit:

the Tower of London, Madame Tussaud's, the London Eye . . . the Trocadero, the list just. . . stops.

But, much as I love my home town, it is regrettably all a bit crap: run as the personal fiefdom of an inveterate publicity addict for close on a decade, central London has extra-long buses that carry approximately the same amount of passengers as the double-deckers that they replaced – but in twice the amount of road. Because payment for these buses works on an ill-conceived honour system, virtually no one pays for their ticket except slow-witted out of towners. The net result is a bus system crippled by dwindling revenues and new, unbelievably expensive vehicles that have effectively doubled the traffic congestion in the West End. It has long been quicker to walk the length of Oxford Street rather than take the bus. It's now quicker to ride a sled dragged by sloths (I've checked), and you're less likely to be exposed to an incessant din of tinny hip-hop played through a mobile phone speaker which robs it of its enjoyably visceral beats and just leaves the cretinously homophobic and racist lyrics intact.

In addition, because of an interminably Orwellian succession of terror alerts, we have few if any litter bins on any of the tube or train stations. The outcome is a calf-deep drift of free newspapers and discarded fried chicken that provides a perfect habitat for rats, fleas and, for all I know, eels. Our vagrants are renowned as the most insistently professional in the known world, following the naive tourist from hotel lobby to overpriced identikit

West End show and back with a well-rehearsed story that only the price of a rock of crack can silence.

Of course London is no more dirty, disorganised or unpleasant to visit than any city you might care to mention – it's just the one I know best. I've learned to endure its vicissitudes by dint of a lifetime's experience in much the same way as you, dear reader, may well have come to tolerate the weaknesses of Birmingham, Newcastle or perhaps even Milton Keynes. Wherever we may be, that's the environment we're adapted for: don't try to fight evolution.

THINGS THAT DO NOT MIX #2:
Sunburn and baths

Increasingly, British citizens are subject to metering of their water supply, either to preserve a valuable natural resource or to increase the revenue of companies run by former schoolmates of prominent MPs, depending on your level of cynicism. Consequently, we tend to take fewer baths, making the morning commute an even more noisome and unpleasant business than one might expect of the inadequate and shoddy transport services provided by companies run by former schoolmates of prominent MPs. Thus, when on holiday and faced with a capacious bath ready to be filled to the brim with someone else's water, it's quite natural that we will run ourselves the deepest, hottest, bubbliest bath we can. As indeed we should. Few other countries seem to be as arid as our permanently rain-sodden and flood-prone homeland, because the same constraints regarding water seem not to apply elsewhere around the globe. One word of warning, though: if you've been in the sun all day and are planning to wash off the accreted sand, sweat and suntan lotion which has crusted itself on your skin, check carefully for any sign of sunburn before you leap in. Too precipitous an entry into a 100 °F jacuzzi will, without doubt, elicit from you a scream of surprise and outrage they will be able to hear in Oldham.

The secret pleasure that does not speak its name, but just listens quietly

There are fewer entertainments more economical, entertaining or possessed of such infinite variety as eavesdropping: even completely fictitious eavesdropping experiences, like soap operas, the once very popular *Big Brother* television show or SETI command immense interest.

The thing is, eavesdropping is only any fun if you've got some idea what the person you're earwigging is talking about. If people are barking away in German or Arabic or some other godforsaken noise, there's really no joy to be extracted from their private conversations at all. No amount of leafing through your phrase book is going to help: you want to hear about extramarital affairs, drug deals, and family feuds, not listen to people v e r y s l o w l y book a table in a restaurant.

There are, admittedly, other English-speaking countries. Australia comes to mind, although only briefly, because it's so far away and full of snakes. Spain is (increasingly) another. The only place you're really guaranteed to hear some prime quality gossip, though, is in your own backyard*. Which is also, you'll be pleased to hear, very easy to get to.

International football: The quest for pies

In August 2005, the *Scotsman* reported, with a commendable lack of irony, that eight supporters were hacked to death at a 'Play for Peace' football friendly in Haiti. Now, I'm not suggesting, if you travel abroad to attend a European club match, that you will meet a similar fate,

---

* Because then there's at least half a chance that you'll know one of the *dramatis personae* and every chance that you'll comprehend the peculiarly idiomatic style of speech in which gossip is characteristically delivered.

but certainly there are crucibles of hate, like the Galatasaray ground, where you may be temporarily distracted from the quality of play by the sheer volume of abuse (and, indeed, pints of Turkish urine) that will be hurled at you as the match progresses.

Any nostalgic notion you may entertain of standing on the terraces with a thermos of Bovril will have been beaten out of you long before you even consider travelling to an away match, but even the traditional mystery meat pie is an unattainable dream at Continental grounds. If your side are lucky enough to draw Slovan Bratislava, you might muddle through with their steak sandwich, and Dutch and Belgian sides can at least offer a reasonable portion of chips, but in the main you're going to be faced with a confusing range of oddities when all you want is some slaughterhouse sweepings in a thick and manly crust. You're probably best off transferring to a team that aren't going to be booking too many European fixtures, Celtic perhaps? Their shirts are lovely.

Now that's what I call a holiday: Chucking a sickie

There are few pleasures so delicious, or so economical, as chucking a sickie: for the price of a simple telephone call, wherein you demonstrate the dramatic talent that, but for the siren call of a glamorous career in the financial services industry, would have seen you treading the boards at the Old Vic, you buy yourself a day's liberty to live the Playboy lifestyle in your own home. Computer games (I recommend a gentle session of *Unreal Tournament* for the convalescing office drone), magazines you never normally have time to read and curious arena-style talk shows where fishwives bark at each other for no clear reason – all these are laid before you like some grand buffet of indulgence. The truly talented thespians among you will leave the Hoover out in a way that suggests an intention to clean and pull off a convincing sneeze or two as your loved one returns from a hard day's work. The result? A nice evening on the sofa with a blanket over your legs and every possibility of some chicken soup for supper.

Contrast this idyllic experience with the misery of even a mild cold on holiday. If you've elected to go on holiday in the UK, you can at least buy some Lemsip and hole up in your cottage, but with no computer and the inferior television that owners of holiday let properties always seem to think will suffice, you'll soon reach the limits of your patience. Overseas things get even worse, with none of the familiar remedies visible on the shelves of the local *supermercado* (how our Continental cousins survive without the minty wonderment of Buttercup syrup I will never know) and the relentless reminders that you're on holiday and, therefore, under some obligation to do stuff and not just slack about replacing the solicitous chicken broths of home.

When you consider the enhanced misery of vacation illness and the additional opportunities for contracting mild ailments – food poisoning, heat prostration, Ebola – while you're on holiday, and then remember that you can't call in to the travel company and explain in a theatrically croaky voice that you're a bit under the weather and so won't be on holiday today (thus lengthening your overall stay), it *almost* seems as if the whole holiday enterprise isn't worth the risk.

Another annoying thing you probably hadn't thought of . . .

Be ye male, or be ye female, there is no doubt that your skin will periodically be disfigured by the odd spot. It's all part of the 'intelligent design' of mankind. You never see a leopard with a spot, do you? Well, not *that* kind of spot. Evolving in parallel to our propensity for zits, though, is a winning way with chemicals that has culminated in a wide range of concealers to suit every skin tone. Virtually every woman in Britain, and more men than you might think, have availed themselves of these flesh-tinted wonder pastes.

The things is, when we go away on holiday, all the rich food and complimentary *digestifs* we consume have the effect of promoting more of these spots than might be considered usual, and, more importantly, at the exact same moment as all the extra sun is darkening our skin so that the concealer we have carefully chosen in Boots to match our pasty fifty-weeks-of-the-year complexion now highlights rather than conceals the offending eruptions. Let's hope you weren't hoping to pull while you were away.

You might, by this time, be thinking that I've got some idea that going on holiday is just one bloody annoying thing after another. You're right, I have. And I'm trying to give it to you.

So you're in economy: What the aircrew *really* think of you

You may fleetingly believe, as the sleekly androgynous sky-drone greets you on boarding, that you are a valued customer of Cheapo Air PLC, and that the aircrew are so keen to attend to your every whim as you fly economy to Ibiza, Orlando or perhaps Nice (as long as, of course, it involves peanuts, volcanically hot chicken dinners or disappointingly weak gin and tonics). You should disabuse yourself of this idea by the time you have buckled yourself into your seat and pulled the slightly tattered looking catalogue of perfumes and novelty bears from the seatback pouch. You are cargo. A particularly annoying sort of cargo that, unlike more tractable loads, like Zimbabwean plums or grey import iPods, demands weak gin and tonics every now and then in a most annoying way.

Detracting from your already piteously low approval rating is the possibility that you are one of the thousand or so numpties a year who feel that they should succumb to 'air rage'. Air rage is one facet of a mass hysteria that has its principal transmission vectors in tabloid newspapers. It also manifests itself in assorted food intolerances and allergies, all of which defy modern medicine, which is short-sightedly focused on detecting and eradicating actual real diseases. Like Myanmar and Mumbai, it used to have a better, more memorable name that everyone understood. It used to be called 'weak gin-induced acting the tit' and had a simple remedy that generally involved a stern talking to. Nowadays persons acting the tit on aeroplanes are significantly more likely to be Tasered than talked to. It's one of the very few things we can thank those fine people at Al Qaeda for.

I'm not complaining, they probably *should* be Tasered (and often), it's just that, because aircrew are trained to be constantly on the lookout for these 'air ragers', they have downgraded their already brusque service standards in order to spend more time being vigilant etc. If you're content to be suspicious cargo, then I suppose that's your own affair, but personally I would rather travel in a way that guaranteed me decent treatment and the appropriate respect for a gentleman of my station. As there are currently no methods of travel which can guarantee these niceties, I elect, therefore, not to travel at all. I urge you to join me.

Why enjoy the comfort of your own home when you can get someone else in to do that for you?

If you're an average homeowner, you're probably shelling out the best part of a thousand quid a month in mortgage payments. If you're going to go away for two weeks, you're not *exactly* throwing half a month's money away – after all, you need to keep your house to store all the things you forgot to pack, for one thing – but wouldn't it be nice, if you could somehow make that £500 work for you? Wouldn't it be great if you could find a nice family that lived somewhere you wanted to go and temporarily swapped houses with them for a fortnight?

No, it wouldn't.

Even after you've spent the weekend before you go away cleaning the house from top to bottom twice because, before you leave, you don't want to be thought of as a gang of slovens by the virtual strangers you're swapping with and twice when you get back because you're afraid they might have brought Cuban dust mites with them, you've still got the problem of placing a last-minute call to your home contents insurers who, of course, will have no intention of honouring any claim made for that irreplaceable picture of your grandparents that inexplicably looked like the ideal toy snowboard to a twelve-stone eight-year-old from Florida who was buzzing off his moobs on unfamiliar confectionery.

Then there's the car. Hire cars are fumigated with noxious industrial-strength air freshener for a reason: you really don't want to lower your rear end into the vast Yucatan crater made in the driver's seat by your American counterpart knowing that several cubic tonnes of holiday food fart gas has been trapped in the upholstery. That's if they don't ding the paintwork by driving on the wrong side of the road or trying to squeeze your motor into one of Britain's special nanotechnology parking spots.

As a bonus, you'll still be finding jewellery, drugs and bank statements you hid from prying eyes months later. If you really wanted to stay in a nice family home, with all the comforts you're used to, then why don't you just . . . Oh! They left you a £3.99 bottle of wine? That makes it all OK then.

THINGS YOU CAN ONLY DO @ HOME #15: Pottering around in the garden

The great thing about gardening is, no one really knows how to do it. You get the occasional bluffer on the telly or the radio cracking on like they've got an idea, but their advice always seem to boil down to 'cut it off, it'll grow back', which is the same specious logic that makes people buy those home haircutting kits or consider circumcision.

Because no one can definitively tell you aren't doing it properly, gardening is quite edifying, even for a dilettante like me, and as long as you remember that one man's weedy lawn is another man's meadow*, and there are never any wrong answers, it's quite a tranquil business. All you need to really get into it is a couple of weeks in the garden, preferably in the summer when the weather's not too bad. Just hack the ends of a couple of the bigger plants, empty some of those envelopes you bought down the garden centre into the dirt, and sit back in a deckchair and admire your handiwork. A gin and tonic will top the sense

---

* Which, once you think about it, is the root of the creeping moral relativism that's eroding our way of life. Perhaps we should ban *Gardeners' Question Time*?

of achievement off nicely. Beats any package tour you can name hands down.

Florida: In the country of the bland, the dead-eyed mouse is king

Florida is an almost entirely useless appendage that dangles from the bottom of the United States like a eunuch's wedding tackle. Traditionally home to alligators and a few enterprising inbreds, it was latterly reinvented as a vast swampy retirement home to which youthful thrusting Americans could banish those relatives who had carelessly allowed themselves to get old, and then co-opted as the de facto capital of the Mickey Mouse empire. It seems to me entirely just that the state most directly responsible for electing George W. Bush to the presidency of the USA will continue to pay the price for his refusal to sign the Kyoto accords long after the clownish glove puppet of the neocon lobby has downsized his operation to a series of decreasingly impressive golf club dinners. Hurricanes of ever more impressive magnitude are going to be slamming into the home of Disney and decrepitude for centuries to come as the effects of American climate vandalism come home to roost. That's just as it should be, just don't let the relentless pester power of your *Pirates of the Caribbean*-obsessed progeny allow it to become your problem.

Travel insurance: Why you need it, why you'll never use it

Going to the dentist is never a particularly enjoyable experience. You can search the seamier suburbs of the Internet all day and not find a single person who derives pleasure from dental treatment. To their credit, dentists do their best to set nervous patients at their ease with the odd encouraging word or Beatles CD. Should you require an emergency filling or replacement crown overseas*, though, you will be denied even these mild palliatives. German dentists don't *actually* say 'Is it safe?' while they're drilling your teeth, but they might as well, quite honestly. The absence of a common language reduces the transaction to the level of a carpenter and a piece of wood, with you in the role of the unhappy timber. Also, CDs of

---

* And bear in mind that dental hygiene is one of those things that tends to slip when you're on your holidays. The absence of a routine can derail a strict flossing regime within a day or two and, once that's combined with a steady diet of baklava, you're into a world of hurt, soldier.

oompah music aren't as relaxing as our Teutonic cousins think they are.

Every implement that the dentist puts in your mouth has a wickedly curved hook on the other end, which wiggles about in front of your eyes and is there exclusively to remind you not to fidget. That's part of the terror of the dentist and we accept that. The same pointy hook wiggling action underscored with a running commentary in German (or, indeed, any language with which we have only a passing acquaintance) is a more profoundly affecting torment before which the stoutest soul might quail.

At least when it comes to dentistry one has the advantage of being able to comprehend (more or less) what is going on. Should you have the misfortune to prang a rented scooter in the Canaries, or upend a quadbike in the Caribbean, you may require less familiar therapies, which you may well find even more stern muttering in unfamiliar tongues while people stitch, snip and otherwise repair your extremities. All of this, of course, is very much to be avoided, which is why travel insurance policies always include a provision to repatriate you to the UK as early as possible so that you can contract our Great British MRSA at the taxpayer's expense rather than be left in an expensive foreign hospital where you are in danger of adversely affecting the insurers' profitability. That's why we buy travel insurance. We know that the very best medical professionals have very widely elected to leave their various countries to live and work in the UK and so, when one of us suffers some mishap, the last thing we want is to be treated by whoever's left. We want to go home.

The magical thing about travel insurance is, although everyone buys it, only a small number of people could actually put their finger on where their documentation might be if the reps announced a sudden travel insurance document-themed quiz. Add the distraction of an abscessed gum or sprained ankle into the equation and that small number moves close to zero. People only buy travel insurance as a last minute panic thing, usually by looking at the websites of a huge number of effectively indistinguishable providers in a relatively short time. This makes it very hard to remember which one they actually went with in the end, let alone how to contact them or what the policy number might be, so very few claims are ever made. That magic makes the sale of travel insurance one of the most hilariously profitable businesses of all time. Why not buy some today?

How the office temp will undermine you while you're away

Everyone makes the extra effort to make a good impression in that early honeymoon period between acceptance letter and first appraisal. After that most normal people settle into a relaxed routine of wandering in a few minutes late, putting in a solid couple of hours on eBay and Facebook until it's time for lunch, and then popping out for a leisurely pub lunch before ambling back to the office to pick up their bag and go home. That's just as it should be: if everybody worked at full capacity all the time, our economy would overheat dangerously, causing all sorts of unpleasantness and upset in the Nikkei, the Dow Jones and that other one . . . the knapsack?

The thing is, temps are always on honeymoon: that extra few pence an hour they get is supposed to cover the lack of pension and holiday pay but, because they are agents of Satan, they tend to spend it instead on biscuits for everyone in the office and fresh flowers for the reception area. The net result is, everybody loves them. The bastards.

So when you get back after two weeks of pony trekking in Snowdonia or whatever it might be, it's not so much that everyone's forgotten you and what job it was you actually *did* (although that may also be the case for the less effectual reader), it's just that everyone really liked the temp and wants them back instead of you.

Which is a fairly galling notion, considering that you didn't really want to go on holiday anyway and fell off the horse twice. Perhaps a series of shorter breaks closer to home might have kept you in the public eye more effectively, proven more economical and provided more sustained respite from the arduous business of messing around on eBay and Facebook?

How to turn dirt into money

Those who can't do, teach. Similarly, land that can't do anything else is a golf course. If you own a good-sized chunk of dirt that won't grow anything and nobody wants to live on, then you're generally advised to turn it into a car park. If it isn't near anything that anyone wants to get to, though, then it's hard to persuade anyone to pay good money to park on it. That's when you hook up a network of sprinklers to squirt more water than you'd like the millions of people affected by drought in the horn of Africa to ever hear about and call the resultant patch of grass a golf course.

There are quite a few people in the world who are immensely keen on golf. More than a few of those are willing to pony up a tidy sum to spend a couple of weeks whacking a smallish ball around. Put enough of them on your over-irrigated patch of dirt and you've got yourself a tidy little revenue stream. Of course you'll need to add in a few basic amenities to amuse the golfers' wives and children, who would have preferred something more in the traditional plangent ocean/damp sand/thick paperback line. These amenities can be pretty low-end, after all they'll have paid up long before they realise that the nearest non-golf amusement is an invigorating ten-minute walk from the flimsily-constructed cabañas. And here's the beauty part: Golf (and indeed tennis, tetris, or tic-tactoe) pros in your punters' local clubs tend to be embittered souls who had their childhood dreams of stardom snatched away when they realised that they would never achieve the top flight of sporting success. What makes it worse for them is they have to hold back when playing against paying customers for fear of disheartening them and endangering next month's membership fees. Not so for the elite team of second-raters you will recruit for your golf resort: they can humiliate their opponents as much as they like. After all, with your ramshackle chalets and motorway services-quality catering, they won't be re-booking for next year anyway.

THINGS THAT
DO NOT MIX #3:
The seaside and geometry

Virtually every pop science book since *A Brief History Of Time* has included a reference to Edwin Abbott Abbott's celebrated Victorian mathematical fantasy, *Flatland*. It's frequently used as an entry point for study of higher-dimensional geometry by introducing to us 3D people hypothetical lower-dimensional beings existing in 2D or even 1D worlds. The same understanding could be achieved by visiting any coastal resort: the chief recreation in most seaside towns is one-dimensional, consisting of walking along the beach or promenade for an arbitrary distance, and then retracing one's steps. Less ambitious coastal holidaymakers identify one point on the plane bounded by the promenade, sea and any two groynes and remain there until they are sufficiently cold or sunburned to beg readmittance to their B&B. Bolder, or more desperate, pleasure seekers might venture into the second dimension of a road slightly further inland that runs parallel to the promenade, studded with dozens of near-identical shops selling the same few products: buckets and spades (traditional), windbreaks (essential), inflatable water craft (suicidal) and so forth. Certainly, if you've undertaken this jaunt with children and neglected to bring them suitable footwear, a set of paper flags of the British nations or a disappointingly fragile plastic windmill, you'll be grateful for the presence of this parade of tat emporia.

There's another feature common to every coastal resort, whether we're talking about Torbay, Thessaloniki or a (if the weather continues to go mental) newly-flooded Timbuktu: the kayak family. I think it's always the same family, probably working for some particularly specialist guidebook, and they're going to ruin every beach holiday for the rest of time. Kayaking around like a demographically correct Flying Dutchman with the buddingly fruity teenage girl sitting behind her suspiciously 1950s looking dad and the perfectly tanned skinny son and pleasantly plump mother bringing up the rear, they are a physical manifestation of everything you're not: wholesome, well-adjusted and with a taste for outdoorsy pursuits like, well, like kayaking, for a start. If you're trying to introduce a much-needed third dimension to the holiday by skimming stones off the plane of the ocean's surface (or, if we're still in Timbuktu, off an especially flat sand dune) they will be there with their bloody kayak, quacking away to each other in Received Pronunciation about how absolutely fucking super it all is and distracting you from the exacting calculation of angles of incidence that, after all, nearly stumped the fearsomely brainy designers of the bouncing bomb. If you angle it just right, you might just catch one of them in the temple with an especially flat stone and still make it look like an accident. Even if you don't get away with it, at least our fine modern prisons are 3D.

The Lonely Planet code: Understanding guidebooks

The thing you have to remember about guidebooks, except for this one, obviously, is that the people who write them *really like going on holiday*. This can make them a trifle optimistic about the quality of the experience. Also, when they're not writing about the more standard sorts of holiday that us ordinary people might accidentally end up on, they're off doing the really weird adventure stuff for people who are planning to have a crap time on purpose. This rather skews their findings away from the 'having a nice rest and maybe the odd pub lunch' ideal of regular fellows like you and me and somewhat towards the 'leaving a colossal pile of litter at the base of Chomolungma* ideal' of foolish young men with ice in their beards. The goggles they wear up those mountains are pretty rose-tinted: after brewing up tea in a snowbound tent at 27,700 feet, the surliest Athens *taverna* owner will seem to be offering 'friendly service' and even the most woefully appointed Loire valley campsite will seem 'clean and well-equipped'. It's worth remembering. When you're reading a Duff Guide to somewhere-or-other, ratchet your expectations down a notch or two, then tear out a few pages and Sellotape in a couple of pages from this book. Then read it again. Then, at least if you *do* end up on holiday, you won't be too disappointed.

* It's what we're supposed to call Everest now. You know, like Bombay or Peking (but of course bear in mind they both still have their ducks). Although Sir George Everest pronounced his name Eee-vrest anyway. And, for that matter, Robert Louis Stevenson pronounced Doctor Jekyll 'Jeee-cull'. And while we're on the subject, Kipling always thought of Mowgli as 'Mau-glee'. You see? This *is* quite a useful and interesting book after all!

Pleasures rare and sublime: The long lie-in, the siesta and the early night

(a) **The Lie in:** One of the greatest pleasures known to the working man (and even a few working women), the lie-in is generally confined to one weekend morning – typically a Sunday out of some atavistic allusion to our country's Christian past when we honoured Our Lord's well-deserved, although disappointingly newspaperless, lie-in after that very first working week. One might imagine that the lie-in might be a more frequent feature of a holiday fortnight, but for reasons that defy understanding, it's a pleasure all too often denied to the hapless holidaymaker by the tyrannical martinets of the hotel kitchen, with their unreasonably strict breakfast time cut-off. Even if one *can* bring oneself to pass up the cornucopia of slightly stale croissants and Lilliputian pots of jam, there is always the matter of the inevitable mild ache in the lower back, which might hopefully be ascribed to an unfamiliarly soft mattress, but equally could be the onset of holidaymakers' alcohol-based kidney failure necessitating at least one big glass of water. The tiny glass provided for tooth-cleaning operations is generally too small to be filled and taken back to bed for adequate kidney therapy, which requires the thirsty hypochondriac to stand on the cold bathroom tiles for long enough to ruin any intended lie-in.

(b) The Spanish may have a word for it, but the **after-lunch snooze** is one of the rarest joys in any language. Most nations have sacrificed the siesta as part of the price of modern civilisation, with work now continuing more or less throughout the daylight hours, making the luxury of a post-prandial rest only the province now of people who have elected to make no material contribution to our great society: the long-term unemployed, royal personages, authors of fairly droll books about travel and so forth. A short post-meridian kip is also the natural companion to the pub lunch, which, in our needlessly materialistic world, is itself a pleasure now confined to the weekend. So of course, like many of the finer things in life, one might reasonably expect to have the odd afternoon *schluf* when on holiday. Regrettably this is not as easily done as said: British bed and breakfast establishments, for example, seem to have a puritanical expectation for residents to be out of the building for much of the day, soaking up the gentle drizzle for which our seaside resorts are justly famed ('so bracing!'). Even when beyond the reach of Cromwellian seaside landladies, the designated driver of the party will frequently bridle at holiday time perceived as wasted and will be constantly chivvying at their more *relaxed* fellow travellers to get out and see the Acropolis or Euro Disney or some other godforsaken horror. There is one place you can get a decent midday sleep, though. I bet you can guess where it is too. I'm willing to gamble that wherever you live there's an agreeable little pub not more than ten minutes walk from your house and that, once they get over the shock of seeing you in there on a Wednesday lunchtime, the licensees will be happy to rustle you up a fine roast or, at the very least, pull a packet of peanuts from their soft porn cardboard placard. There you can while away a convivial hour or two with some horse racing flickering gently on a muted television like the comforting fire which warmed and protected our cave-dwelling forebears before ambling home, flopping into your own bed and rising refreshed at about sixish with the whole evening still ahead of you.

(c) **The Early night:** An act which, in normal life, seems an admission of defeat, suggesting that you're not quite up to the fast pace of modern life and so will have to record *The Sopranos* and go to bed as soon as the kids are asleep, becomes a yet stronger temptation when you're on holiday and there's nothing on telly except some rather puzzlingly shouty Italian game shows anyway. But you're on holiday, and sleeping through it would be a waste. As if you could: there's always a group of teenagers on every campsite or chalet farm who turn up with one acoustic guitar but somehow manage to create an apocalyptic row that makes the artillery barrages of the Somme seem like easy listening. Even when the flamenco terrorists do succumb to Morpheus, there's still the matter of the crickets. Crickets seem to live more or less everywhere that Britain isn't, and make a scarcely believable racket which makes sleep anywhere between the tropics of Cancer and Capricorn an unattainable fantasy throughout the summer months. Our Continental cousins are, of course, well aware of this, which is why they choose to retaliate to the incessant chirping with an infuriating racket of their own. This battle has been raging nightly since the end of the last Ice Age. Perhaps, if we give it a little longer, a clear victor will emerge. Until then, best find somewhere to sleep that sounds a little more like home.

The longest day: Getting back to work

If there's any one thing worse than going on holiday, it's coming back. The unfamiliar struggle into 'real' clothes after a fortnight in sarongs and the soul-pulverising Monday morning queue for a season ticket are bad enough, but once you've eventually remembered the way back to work and pushed aside the snowdrift of accumulated post from your desk, there will be the apparently interminable parade of people telling you that you don't look very brown and that they've had a heatwave while you've been away. A meagre Pret à Manger sandwich will barely touch the sides after weeks of rich holiday food and the residual blood poisoning from a fortnight's worth of long boozy lunches will finally come home to roost around 3-ish. You will just about feel normal by five, in time for the grim realisation that *it's heads down now until Christmas* to descend on

you much as a Turkish cleaner's clog might descend upon
an unwary cockroach in an unsanitary holiday bungalow.
Whatever fleeting pleasure you may have experienced
while you were away, it isn't worth this. But all that's for
another book . . .

Acknowledgements

It's hard to imagine that I'd have even finished any kind of book without the unvarying patience of my lovely wife Cassie, the indefatigable enthusiasm of my agent, Susan Smith, and the support, guidance and tolerance of Rowan Yapp, James Spackman and all their pals at John Murray. Tom Bromley and Simon Trewin are responsible for getting me started in this caper, and I'd like to thank them for that, even if you wouldn't. I should also thank Tom Whitwell and my many other my friends and colleagues at *The Times*, who have had to endure me testing various bits of this book out on them while they were trying to write important news stories. My in-laws, the Chaddertons, provided invaluable help and succour when I was investigating matters Iberian. Special mention should be made of my daughter Leah Moran, who accompanied me on much of the gruelling research for this volume, which involved attending a dangerously slapdash Spanish Circus.

For extra content, related news items, research notes, and the bits that weren't good enough to go into the book go to www.SodAbroad.com